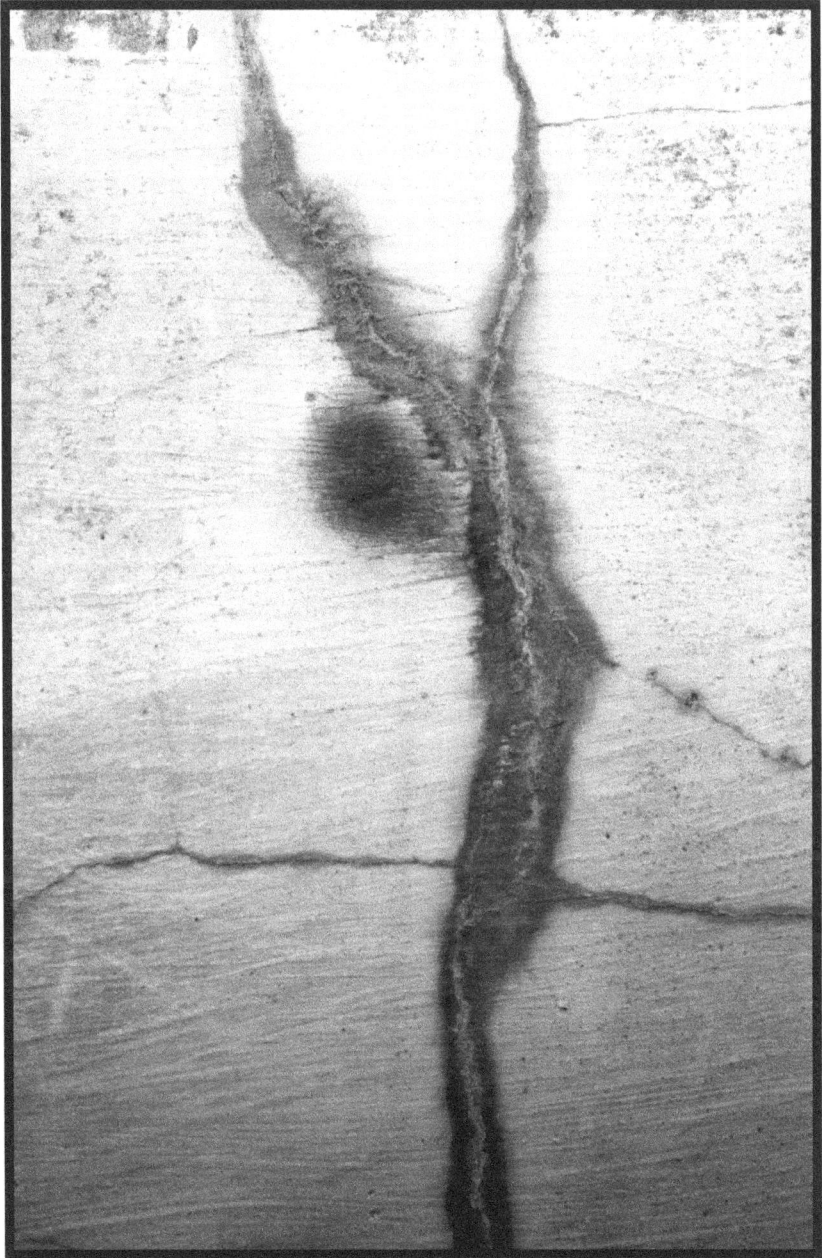

Gutters & Alleyways

Perspectives on Poverty

and Struggle

Edited by

Nancy Lynée Woo & Sarah Thursday

Lucid Moose Lit

Lucid Moose Lit engages the literary arts with social justice issues.

The mission of Lucid Moose Lit is to be an activist press with a clear goal: improve the state of the world for humans, animals and ecosystems by welcoming multiple perspectives on controversial topics. We aim to be inclusionary by bringing different views together in productive conversation.

LUCID MOOSE LIT
poetry with purpose

Copyright ©2014
ISBN-13: 978-0692284568
ISBN-10: 0692284567
Lucid Moose Lit
LucidMooseLit.com
Long Beach, CA

In collaboration with:

SADIE
GIRL
PRESS

Cover art, opening photo "Lift," and section photography "Food," "Shelter," "Money," "Tribe," "Soul" by: Mick Victor
www.mickvictor.com

Table of Contents

Part Two: Shelter

Part Three: Money

Part Four: Tribe

Part Five: Soul

Introduction

Welcome, dear readers, to the first incarnation of *Lucid Moose Lit*. Why, you might ask, did we decide to tackle such a heavy topic for our first anthology?

Let's not deny: poverty *is* heavy. It's a burden that many people carry. Here in the United States, about 1 in every 7 people lives in poverty, according to 2013 statistics from the National Center for Law and Economic Justice. The most vulnerable groups are racial and ethnic minorities, women, children and single mothers. According to the same source, 46.5 million people were living in poverty in the United States in 2012—the largest number in the 54 years the Census has measured poverty.

At the time of writing, wealth inequality in the states seems to be getting more pronounced. Even those who never thought they would be susceptible may discover themselves one paycheck away from disaster. Our country is flooded with the debris from the American Dream, and still, global poverty is another beast altogether.

As we first began to compile this collection, we wanted to ask, what is poverty? What does it look like, feel like, taste like, smell like—who are the human beings behind the word? And what do we do about it? What *can* we do about it?

Poverty can take a myriad of different faces, and "it" often lives invisibly—or near invisibly—just around the corner from egregious wealth. Both editors have had their run-ins with the dark side of destitution, and we know how eclipsing it can be. Sarah spent years of childhood moving from city to city and couch to couch, oftentimes not sure where her next bed or meal would come from. Nancy's parents passed on to her patterns born from immigrant struggle and single mother parenting.

Many of the best people we know have also faced their share of serious hardship. Yet, many of us find it hard to talk about—perhaps we feel shame and guilt for not being able to meet the needs of ourselves or our dependents. Oftentimes, we feel crushed by the mounting obstacles that stand before us, always a to-do list of near impossible "things we need to do or have" to even begin climbing out of the rut. Fighting the current alone can seem overwhelming.

But many hands make light work. Many voices make a chorus. Perhaps even many choruses make a movement. As they say, it takes a village to raise a child—and it takes a community to improve social welfare. To start, we believe poems can be little lessons in empathy that want to be shared. For those who have been lucky enough to have never worried about where they're going to sleep, what they're going to eat, or how they're going to escape, thank you for taking the time to listen.

No social issue has an easy or direct solution. Yet, if one person is inspired to action, others will follow. As one of Nancy's teachers said, "All it takes is one loony and a believer." We hope that this book may help inspire the loonies and believers to take a physical step in their own communities. Nancy, a volunteer on the grassroots level, and Sarah, a teacher working with low-income communities, have seen the amazing things that can be accomplished when people work together.

Listen. Talk. Act.

And if you think that by reading this book, or volunteering in your neighborhood, or organizing a community action group, or simply listening to a friend, doesn't have much of an impact, take a moment to remember how intricately connected we all are.

> A man, while walking along the beach, sees hundreds of sea stars that have recently washed up onto the shore. As he wonders what might have happened, he sees a child in the distance, throwing the sea stars back into the ocean, one by one. When the man reaches the child, he says, "There are hundreds and you're just a kid. There's no way you could possibly make a difference." The child throws another sea star into the ocean, and says, "I made a difference to that one." Then the child picks up two more, handing one over to the man.
> –Anonymous

We each have the power to influence the world in a positive direction. The solution begins with a conversation. We sincerely thank you for taking this journey with us.

With warmth and love,
Nancy Lynée Woo and Sarah Thursday
Lucid Moose Editors

Part One: Food

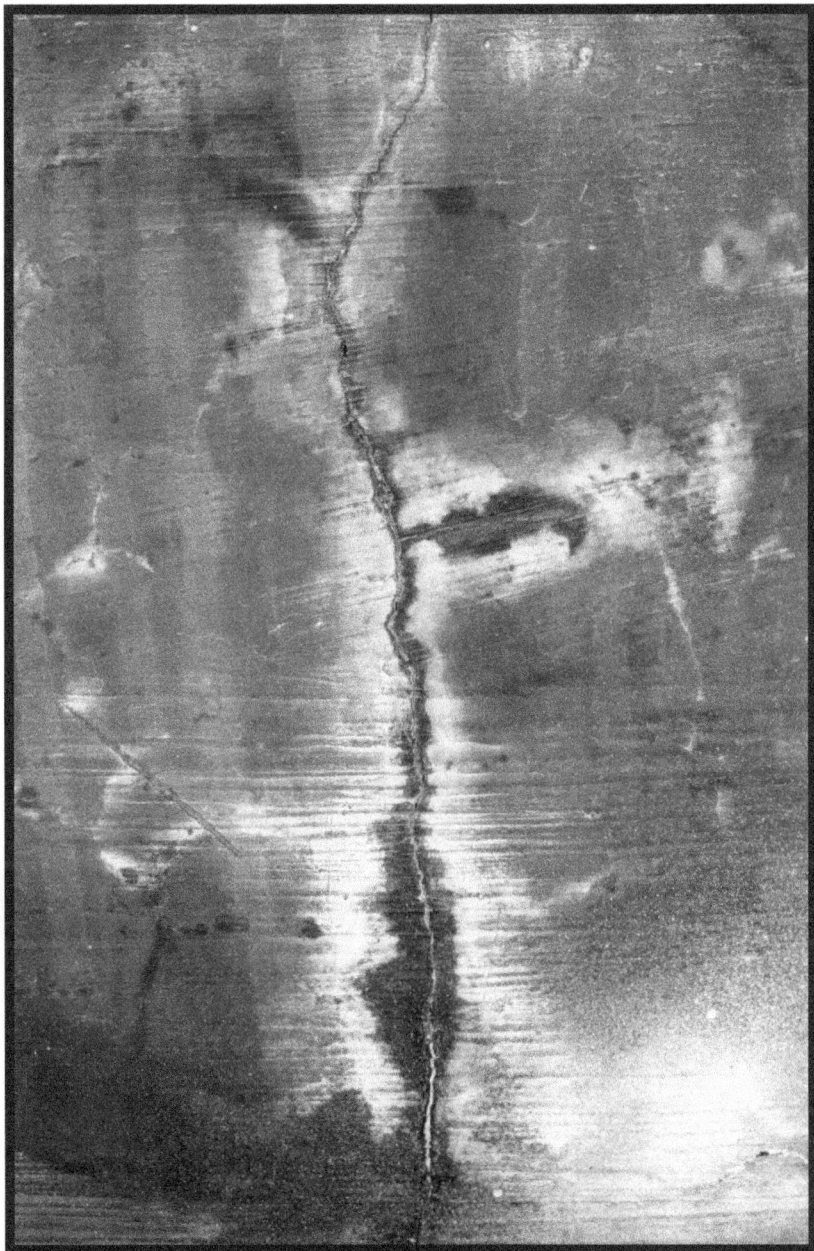

Yvonne M. Estrada
In the Balance

In dark blue dawn downtown
a man asks for change.
My seven-year-old son watches
me dig in a pocket.
He asks "Why did you give
him money?"
I hold my breath
while answers slide off
the heap of reasons
I could use to explain
charity, poverty, loss,
do unto others, or karma.
His perfect needs-to-know face waits.
I check with the sky,
6:00 a.m. and Morning Star
holds a cosmic scale,
in one pan are gas station, old muscle car,
mother and son;
the other pan will be filled
with the words I say,
destitute people my son
will encounter, and future actions
he will take.
My response rushes out with my exhalation,
"Because he doesn't have any, and we do."
He nods like a monk,
absorbs the weight
of this. I watch him change,
his young heart expands,
and his world levels out
for a time.

Alexis Rueal
Grocery Shopping

Mamma says we have to get there before the bleach.
Get there right after the stock boys go back inside,
after they finish smoking.
I wonder if they smell like Mamma,
I don't like how she smells after she smokes.

Mamma says the food will still be fresh.
They forgot the bleach this time;
she says it will be at least 10 minutes
before they remember.
I know 10 minutes.
Mrs. Wilson taught us 10 minutes, last week.
I'll look at the clock in the car for Mamma,
tell her when 10 minutes is up.

Mamma is tall.
She can climb into the dumpster.
She won't let me into the dumpster.
She said the dumpster is no place for me.
She kept the car running, this time.
She just put gas in the car.
It's the first time we've been in the car all week.
Mamma says it's easier to be quick when the car is running.
Don't touch the wheel.
Don't touch Mamma's side of the car.
I know this. Mamma taught me this.

Wait outside the dumpster,
catch what Mamma tosses.
Bread, check the bags.
No rips, not squished. Much.
Mamma doesn't mind if the bread is squished.
She says we can still make sandwiches...they'll just look ugly.
Lettuce, still wrapped.

4

Mamma will still peel back some
the leaves and wash the lettuce.
Mamma likes to be safe.

Hamburger. Mamma always looks at the hamburger real good.
I don't know what good hamburger looks like, yet.
Mamma said she'll teach me.
She didn't like this hamburger.
I really wanted hamburger.

Look at the dates on the plastic.
I know dates, now.
Mrs. Wilson is happy I know my dates,
said I learned them quicker than anyone in class.
Mamma said she was proud of me.
This date was two days ago.
Does that mean the food is old?
Mamma says don't pay attention
to the dates; she knows what food is good.

Cereal, crackers, check the boxes.
Check the bags.
If it's ripped, give it back.
Check the clock.
Eight minutes.
Tell Mamma.
Take the jug of milk.
We don't have to use powdered milk tomorrow.
I don't like powdered milk.

Check the clock.
10 minutes.
"Mamma, it's been 10 minutes."
Mamma is always careful when she climbs
out of the dumpster.

She doesn't want to dent the car hood, again.
She helps me with my seat belt.
I can never get this seat belt buckled.
Mamma tells me it's time to go home and make dinner.
Baloney sandwiches, again.
Mamma tells me she's sorry about the hamburger.
She wanted hamburger, too.

Peggy Dobreer
Girl in the Alleyway

Michael Dwayne Smith
Breaking

That longed-for moment you find something worth
longing for—

mustangs,
half of them angry with moonlight, half
with the metal of sun in their eye.

You grind more of your mother's bones
to powder, for flour and pancake makeup

(you'll light a fire for color)

so you can feed younger brother and sister
then quiet into town
to fetch a doctor and another bottle.

You listen everywhere for words that mean
Corazón,
keep them in your pocket

like the smooth river stones your father gave you
the summer before a knife
opened him naked
to the world for the very first time.

Worry stones he called them, and said just rub
away anxiety or pain, but

the stones changed nothing.

You threw them like ossified prayers at the sky
when he died.

Years ago, before your mother became
part-time work and arthritis and wounded animal
moans in her sleep,

she told stories...
How storms rolled out of heaven across the necks
of rumbling horses

how God wept at the pound of awe in their hooves

unbroken horses with bare backs sweating
ecstatic beasts
stampeding in all directions

beasts you believe now you'll ride and ride and ride,

leaving behind
every childhood story lamed by hunger,

rubbing *Heart* sounds together in your mouth.

Maja Trochimczyk
Peeling the Potatoes

Her Grandma showed her how to hold
the knife, cut a straight, narrow strip,
keeping the creamy flesh nearly intact,
ready for the pot of boiling water.

Don't throw away any food. The old refrain.
*My sisters, Tonia and Irena lived on potato peels
in Siberia.* She's confused. She knows
Ciocia Tonia – glasses on the tip of her nose,
perfectly even dentures – but Irena? Who is that?

They were all deported to Siberia. Not sure how
Irena's parents died – of typhus, or starvation, maybe?
They used to pick through garbage heaps,
look for rotten cabbage, kitchen refuse
to cook and eat. They cooked and ate anything
they found under the snow, frozen solid.

The water's boiling. Babcia guides her hand:
*You have to tilt the cutting board
toward the pot, slide the potatoes in.
Don't let them drop and splash you.*

What happened next? *The orphaned children
went with the Anders' Army and the Red Cross
to Iran, Switzerland, Chicago.* The kitchen
fills with memories. Mist above the stove.
Grandma piles up buttery, steaming,
mashed potatoes on her plate. *Eat, child, eat.*

Ten years later, Aunt Irena came to visit.
She looked like Grandma, only smaller.
Her legs were crooked.

Nandini Dhar
Midday Meal

With a view to boost universalization of Primary Education (class I-V) by improving enrolment, attendance, retention and learning levels of children, especially those belonging to disadvantaged sections and to improve nutritional status of students of primary stage, the Cooked Midday Meal Programme was started in West Bengal in 1100 schools of six districts from January, 2003.

1.

I go to the wrong school—
never enough teachers never enough chalk,
never enough blackboard never enough paper
or even enough benches to sit on. We huddle together,
three grades in a single room. Shouting over each
others' lessons—Shah Jahan's Taj Mahal overlapping
the shape of the earth overlapping some poem.
And that's how, although I'm in class five,

I've made friends with a class four girl.
Who bites her nails, chews the shards
as if they are candies. At the least,
to her, they must be molten molasses.
Yet, they are what they are—pieces
of her own body made unfamiliar
by her tongue. I understand. We talk about
babu bari girls—the ones our mothers hug, feed,
bathe and scold.

For her, I put in words the time when Tumpa, at
whose house my mother works, and I, sat down
to eat. Together. It doesn't happen every day—
yes, it was Tumpa's birthday.
This new friend, silly girl, asks, "what's that?"

I shush her—for, I do not know. I don't have one. And,
        I keep telling her, how Tumpa's mother changed places
        with my ma. Almost. And loaded my plate
with rice, dal, achar, fish and chicken meat. Only
that one time. And, how I had foregone washing
my hand with soap afterwards. How I kept smelling
it hours after – onions, garlic, fish, chicken and mustard oil
mingled into my skin. I hold my hand up
under nail-chewing girl's nose: hoping
my palmlines would remember how it felt to dig

into so much abundance.

2.

We line up to eat thrice a week—*midday meal*
that's the name of it. A name that fills the cheek
and a good thing that is. For what is served cannot fill
our tummies. Which keep on squeaking like new
baby shoes: rice thick enough to kill a grown man on the head.
Dal thin as turmeric sprayed water. The grains,
even if they were there once, hidden inside,
have been ladled to fill the cook's rice-plate.
But, we are not to worry. What has been lost
in the shape of grains, has been refilled by worms
clinging to the rice grains as if they are someone's

last pieces of land.

We dig holes in the rice, draw birds and airplanes
on the banana-leaf plate, our fingertips dipped in dal.
Whatever we make gets erased with every slurp of our lips.
She puts a fingerful of rice in her mouth—
"Ei, take another piece of fish. Do you need more sauce?"

I gulp down my own mouthful. Reciprocate. "Here is a piece
of mutton for you. Dip it in the sauce before teething in."
And that's what we do three times every week—talk up food
that does not exist. Then, the bell rings.
We stop eating, scoop up our banana-leaf plates, lift them
off the floor, fold them in between our palms, toss them
into the dustbin before we wash our hands. From between
the folded leaves and our pals. Drops of dal drip on to
the ground—the color of cat vomit.

G. Murray Thomas
Coins on the Sidewalk

In the U.S., you can always find
        coins on the sidewalk.
Do you automatically pick them up?
Or do you check them first,
nothing less than a quarter
being worth the effort to stoop.
Or, your pockets already full of shrapnel,
will you only bend for a bill,
its denomination hidden,
but perhaps a twenty?

In Peru, the money is almost worthless.
Banks pay 80% interest,
and still do not keep up with inflation
1000 soles do oro –
One thousand gold suns –
is barely worth 50¢ American
But it will still buy you lunch.

In Peru, the slums wade into the Amazon,
and scale themselves,
building their own adobe Andes.
In Peru, the shoeshine boys will not give up,
even if you are wearing sneakers.
In Peru, I saw an old man argue vehemently
with an Uzi-toting soldier,
over a 60¢ train fare.
In Peru, you will not find
        coins on the sidewalk.

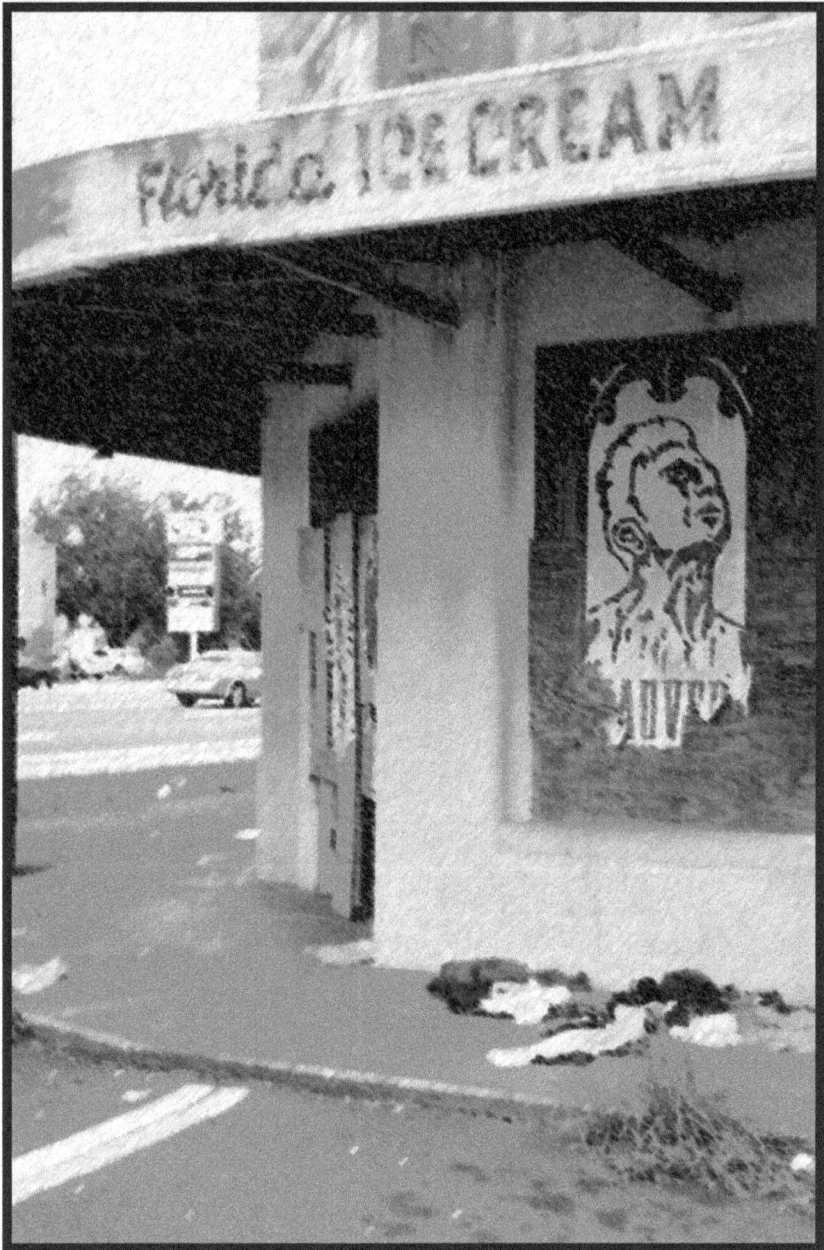

<u>Ginna Wilkerson</u>
Old Drugstore

Trista Dominqu
Leftover Orchard Days

In this city growing up every other
house had a leftover orange, lemon,
avocado, or loquat tree in the back
yard.

We took advantage, pulling the
thousand-seeded orange orbs of
sweet juice from their eaves, making
our way to the brick walls that made
us neighbors, but kept us friends.

Leaving a trail of sweet for the ants to
follow, we sat dangling legs, letting
God's candy dribble down our chins.
Feeling the itch of the peels upon our
lips, we watched as the skins
gathered in piles littering the grass
beneath our feet.

These trees, leftovers from the cities'
orchard days were our summer
snacks when cabinets were bare.
How spoiled we were eating money
that grew from trees, never knowing
how rich we really were.

Robin Dawn Hudechek
Wonder Bread

I must have been about eight or nine
when it appeared on my plate, egg salad
oozing like some sickening daisy-tainted lava,
a molten mass bulging from a pockmarked loaf.
I used to wish it was Wonder Bread
with its pristine whiteness and
oh-so-appealing softness,
bread that could be squeezed between fingers and
flattened smaller than a pencil shaving.
We never knew what was in it, what chemicals
bound its thread of dough so no evidence
could be seen of its molding or rising.
We only knew we couldn't afford it.

Our lunch boxes would never open
like desktops to fanatically ordered desks:
each spine squarely lined to the desk wall
each pencil in its place.
Wonder Bread was like that, and belonged
to a world of tidy certainties, of houses
with predictably manicured lawns, managed
by housewives weeding the sidewalk in a fury,
leaving no dandelions sprouting in hubbed cracks.
I could never understand
why rose bushes were tended with care,
while dandelions were ruthlessly
cut from their growing spaces.

We ate day-old bread
though it never would have been allowed
to take root in any self-respecting grocery bag but ours.

We ate what the other neighbors would have tossed.
I was too young to appreciate
my mother's pride in serving our bread
with its more healthful qualities.
Whole wheat loaves toasted to perfection
in a deliciously warm kitchen,
the windows frosted over
so no one could peer in at us,
elbows shoving playfully, our much-too-loud
voices tipping into laughter, spilling into the room
like milk onto our easy-to-clean plastic table cloths.

Marco A. Vasquez
Over-time

Dad has worked too hard
for too long. Even
when sleeping his eyes
show the constant strain
of squinting the sun
away. He leaves too
early for anybody
to wish him a good
day, watching the sun
rise in his rear-view
mirror. He works
for more than what he
makes and knows it, but he
works. Occasionally
he comes home, lifts me

in his hands—hard
like the paws of a stray
dog—like a sack
of concrete mix and rubs
his seven o'clock
shadow on my face
until I giggle
to tears. Other times, he
gets home after a long
drive filled with brake-lights
and middle-fingers

and a realization
that this is what his
life is all about. He
walks in greeted
with silence, grabs me

with callused claws,
and beats me with the short-
end of his stick until
we feel the same—never
telling me that it hurts him
more than it does me
because I already know
that when I see my skin
bruising, it is his
blood that is clotting.

Jackie Joice
Man with head down in boxing ring

Karla Cordero
A Pig story without Wolf

Home is brick house the
wolf refuses to visit.
She calls me pig.
Mistake out the womb.
Bastard child.
At breakfast Mom serves
a bowl of Cheerios,
glass of orange juice & bleach
to clean out the ugly.
My throat is raw meat, silent
to the taste of broken family.
She scrubs behind ears, sprays
hot water on knees, skin-pieces
run fugitive down drain. *Lucky them.*

I.B. Rad
Two Special Poets

Although Yang Wan-li
was a celebrated Sung poet,
his lesser known wife
also authored lofty sentiments;
for example, at age 70,
when asked
why she rose at daybreak
to make porridge for attendants,
she explained, "It's chilly in the morning
and servants are people too.
Only with warm food in their belly
will they be able to work."

Christina Foskey
Third Degree Burns

Stovetop Ramen cooks my sister's arm pink
her processed ham, mom's slimy entitled child

In the market we shop bottom shelf
reach for dog-food shaped cereal bags

In the kitchen mom's menthols burn grey, unattended
she digs out the bugs growing fat in her skin

No more whole milk from WIC this week
cereal with water again

CPS asks about my sister's arm when it blisters
we tell them it wasn't that bad

Timothy Matthew Perez
it's no wonder inner city kids suffer from ptsd

i breathe through corrupted lungs.

i breathe this corruption into the mouths
of my children.

i cross my arms and watch them choke—

nodding my head at their desperation:
nodding my head at eyes bulging red,

and when they are done choking it down
they wrap arms around my legs and wipe

tears into my knee caps. i shake them loose
like flies, wave them towards a mother

who waits with open arms and pursed lips,

and they float across the room fine as brake dust

and other freeway particles that bounce
along in tiny bits and pieces finding

their way against her—this woman—

who calmly claims me as one of her own, stoic
as a concrete sound barrier that does everything

but keep sound out.

and i wander out the screen door with no screen
and put my ear to the sky like an empty shell

and at every downshifting big rig, at every screeching
wheel, at every hand held too long on the horn . . .

i wait for the crash—no longer breathing but heaving:
trying to catch my breath.

Esmeralda Villalobos
No todo esta perdido (Not all is lost)

Isaac Chavarría
Origins

my father was never
an Aztec

he only sacrificed
himself and
his wife

he struggled
to stay alive
by building
happily-ever-after's
by the block
of ice
en su bebida

y a veces
expressed himself
through random
spousal beatings

he wished to return
to Mexico so much
la frontera became
a mistress

y sus niños
became scattered
mesquite saplings
buscando su origen

Nancy Scott
Afghanistan, 2003
from The Kite Runner

In a dusty village
a man sits in a café smoking
his pipe and drinking tea
from a broken cup.

In his pocket, brass knuckles
he'll use tonight if the boy
he bought with three bags
of rice tries to resist.

Outside an orphanage
on a narrow dirt alley
another man watches over
children playing with sticks

and a wad of cloth, says,
What would you have me do?
The rice will keep the children
alive a few more days.

Joe Gardner
Food Bank

Standing in a long line of shame
a disabled combat vet
and his wife
guiding him
on shaky legs and cane
her arms to support and steady
the years collected in the gray of her hair
the lines on her face
the curled worn hands
that have tended first his mother
to the end
and now him
with what bit of dignity they have left
his proud ball cap VIETNAM VET
her proud husband at her side
his weekly outing
to collect a cruel box of food

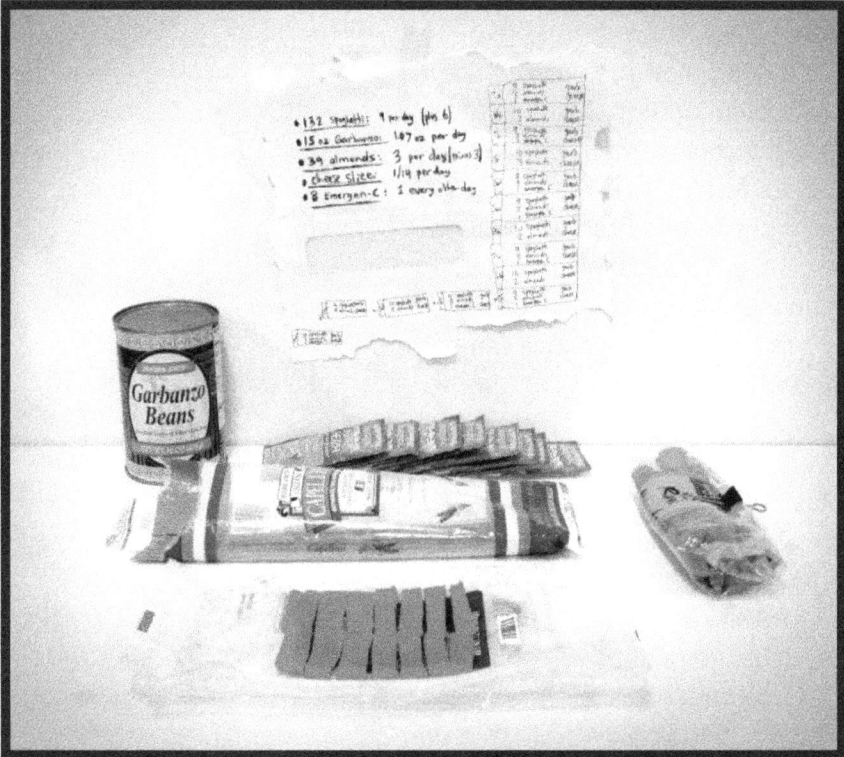

<u>Marc Humpert</u>
Two Week Ration

Loretta Diane Walker
Abundance
after seeing Michael Nye's "About Hunger" exhibition

When life is fissured
like a ripe yellow melon,
and woeful circumstances eat from it
until the soul is a rind of shame,
hunger festers,
becomes a deep brooding wound.

If hunger is darkness, what of light?
Is it like a layer of skin love can put on?
And who can fit such skin,
give a bowl of soup, fist of bread.

I fast to know such darkness;
my tongue is wet with choices,
how can I say,
I know how it feels
to exchange pride for a cookie?

You with begging eyes, cracked skin,
dried mouth, empty hands—
hands now diving in dumpsters, swimming
through a sea of discard,
catching chicken bones—fear.
Forgive me.

I sat down with my full stomach to write
about the sky's generosity last night,
how it opened banks of clouds,
washed the city in relief and when I woke,
my mood rhymed with the color of morning.

I wish my words were seeds;
I wish you could eat them to fill your emptiness.

Tobi Cogswell
Homeless Pete Gets Robbed on Catalina Avenue

It was just a quick cat-nap.
The shady doorway in the alley
behind the stinking hair salon
on Catalina seemed harmless.

He never sleeps longer than 5 or 10,
never at night – bad things happen
with only the giant orange flame
of moon to light a man's dreams.

They took everything–
his radio, his sneakers,
the jacket found in a dumpster
a year ago when some couple

relocating to even warmer
climates cleaned out
their closets. Left with only
the gray sweater tied around

a long-sleeved tee, two pairs
of pants worn one over the other
and a pair of sandals, he's out
asking for a turkey sandwich,

that's all he wants. Just
a little something to stop
the gnawing in his stomach.
He's too empty for grief,
too dignified to smash glass.

Raquel Reyes-Lopez
The Age of Modern Man

It's hard to imagine that not everyone was born into the modern world. At the age of ten, Maria Lopez Gallardo glimpsed contemporary urban society for the first time. Before then, she had lived her entire life in an isolated village in Valle de Michoacán O Campo, Mexico. Her upbringing was like that of a child in an Amish community. However, the villagers she knew did not live their lifestyle by choice. Poverty decided their ways of life for them.

Growing up, Maria lived in a world that most Americans cannot even imagine. In her world, matches lit up the darkness. One match a day would light the firewood in the fireplace. If her family exceeded the one match limit, they wouldn't be able to cook the next day—matches were expensive and each one had to be used wisely. One time, Maria's little sister, Amparo, dropped the match as she was about to light the fire. It was raining, a storm was passing through, and everyone's clothes were damp. That one match could have kept the family warm throughout the night. Instead, Amparo sat with her family by a fireplace filled with wood but no fire. They huddled together, shivering, cold and hungry until morning.

There were other notable differences between village life and a modern lifestyle. Each family member only had two outfits of clothing, but that was the least of their problems. Having food all the time was the difficult part. Maria's family owned one cow and one goat that they milked for fresh milk, a few hens, a rooster, and a pig. However, the cow and goat required a nutrient-dense pasture to produce milk. Rich pasture was sometimes available for them to graze on, and sometimes it was not. The hens also needed food to produce an adequate amount of eggs. The goat needed to grow into adulthood, and then mature to the right age in order to be killed. As for the pig, it took time to fatten for eating. In reality, it was a game of chance. Would food make its way onto their plates or not?

Maria was ten when her mother decided to give her a peek at the modern world. They walked eight hours by foot under the sun to arrive in the city. It was afternoon by the time they got there. Night was closing in and Maria was terrified. The city flared with light. But this light was not from the sun. To Maria, this place was apocalyptic. She began crying and hugged her mother's left leg, reaching for security. Maria pleaded for them to get out of there. Her mother ignored her pleas and took Maria to a family friend's house.

Upon entering the house, Maria was exposed to electricity, a stove, and a television for the first time. Maria was horrified, her eyes swollen from crying so much, and she wanted to escape but couldn't. Her head hurt from looking at the television. She was in shock. No one in her family had prepared her for what was in the city. All she knew was that the television was a box. *How could people possibly be stuck in there and still be alive?* she thought to herself. Electricity was just not natural. She wanted day to be day and night to stay night. The stove, before turning into fire, leaked a horrid odor. She hated how the gas smelled. She wanted to run away and go back to the village. After this visit, like Amish adolescents during rumspringa, Maria became faced with a new life choice: she could either stay in her village community, or move forward with the age of modern man.

After this first exposure to the modern world, Maria went back to the village to live with her grandmother. Her teenage years in village society were difficult. The trouble started when Maria met a boy in the town bakery shop. Her mother forced her to get a job in the city as a housemaid because she hoped that with a job, Maria wouldn't have time for a boy. Maria was only a child at this time, twelve going on thirteen, yet she had a job, and a boyfriend. However, it was normal back then to fall in love at thirteen, and marry at fourteen. There was no law against it in that time; it was nothing out of the ordinary. Eventually, after five miscarriages, she gave birth to her first child.

Maria has seen the advancements of the modern world. She knows that people aren't prisoners of not knowing, aren't left to the dangers of the unknown. There isn't an excuse for ignorance now. Maria also sees the drawbacks of this age. Youth get stunted by using drugs. She sees how we take steps backward together each time the youth get stuck in addiction. Maria believes both the old world and modern world have lessons in their lifestyles. It would be great to incorporate both of them with balance, she thinks. Maria tells me that people are too disconnected from nature in the modern world—something the isolated villager is never disconnected from.

Maria Lopez Gallardo is now a 49-year-old woman living in Montebello, California. Maria left her isolated village in Michoacán O Campo, Mexico, at the age of fourteen. She was shamed and exiled by her mother for kissing her ex-husband in public. Maria has no plans of returning back to her hometown. The last time she visited was in 2006, although she did visit a handful of times before that. I asked Maria one time if she regretted leaving the village she grew up in for her current life. I also asked if she regretted leaving behind her family. Maria frowned at the questions.

"Well, you see, if my exposure to the modern world had never occurred, my answer would be different than the one I am about to give. I don't regret coming into the modern world. As for my family, my mother abandoned me by exiling me. My family is the family I made with my children, grandchildren, and husband here," Maria said.

After she said this, I got up from my chair and gave her a big hug as she cried softly on my shoulder, saddened from recalling her mother's abandonment. Finally, she felt free after vocalizing her struggle. Maria is now remarried; she has two children and two grandchildren. I am proud to say I am one of those children.

Christian Lozada
Hunger Is A Snowflake

I've always been pretty fat,
but my parents have gone without food.
My mom was white-trash hungry,
the embarrassment of food stamps
and proving poverty on a bi-weekly basis.
My dad was third-world hungry;
I have no concept of that horror.
Both of them are driven by past empty stomachs,
ghost pains and scars where no one can see.
So growing up, my brothers and I ate,
pathologically, we ate.
Every morning, after Dad's 7pm to 7am shift,
he'd scream into random fast food microphones:
"give me twelb of the cheep ones."
By "cheep" ones, he meant buck menu burgers
sandwiches
tacos
and every morning, like it was Christmas,
we'd wake up and divvy our shares:
half for breakfast and lunch,
half for dinner.
To this day, mayo doesn't taste right to me
unless it sits out for a day.

If we had leftovers when Dad woke for work,
he would scream about desperation and sacrifice
about love and devotion
about gratitude and hungry days,
days spent begging family and friends for food.
In response, we would eat and cry,
making the salty burgers saltier,
and hope our tears and gratitude would be enough
to ease his once and always hungry stomach.

If it wasn't,
if he still felt slighted,
he would stop bringing home food
to make us feel what he felt
to make us beg friends at school
for the apples and carrots and celery they wouldn't eat.
I would lie to my Muslim friend about pork in his school lunch.
You see, I never went hungry,
but I've woken up to hunger every goddamn day.

Part Two: Shelter

Susan Lefler
Tapping into Loss

You burst into the homeless shelter where you live,
hair plastered to your head, your glasses fogged,
water dripping from your nose, Salvation Army apron

tied around your waist. You've walked three miles
from the store where you rang the bell collecting money
for the poor, your first job in months.

You won't ring the bell for us. You've had enough
of the key of D today, a signature you learned
from the baritone you played in high school band.

I call my friend, a blind musician who has perfect pitch.
He listens to the bells at several stores. They ring
in D, he says, D-Flat, to be exact. The bells

inside me sound a warning, like the tap
of the cane when it meets an obstacle, the tap
on a door to spell out friend, tapping the surface

of a pond to sound the ice. D-flat echoes
as I dodge the aproned stranger who blocks
the entrance to the grocery store, and fail

to add my dollar to his kettle. The insistent tone
in its minor key beats in my ears, the key
of loss—Rigoletto, bent and broken,

the dying swan, marooned in beauty,
trembling in her place, the key
the stars sing into empty space.

Alexis Rueal
The First Night

You try not to think about tomorrow.
You try not to notice the sewer rats in your rest stop bedroom.
Try to block out the fluorescent glow of street lamp midnight.
So you think about your mother.

You try not to notice the sewer rats in your rest stop bedroom.
Your husband, asleep as you remember your shitty choices—
So you think about your mother,
count the ways you will never tell her she was right.

Your husband, asleep as you remember your shitty choices—
remember telling your mom he loved you most of all.
Count the ways you will never tell her she was right;
beg God forgive your painting her a bitch with your tongue.

Remember telling your mom he loved you most of all—
when you were a cocky 20, owning six trash bags and pride?
Beg God forgive your painting her a bitch with your tongue.
Turn the car off so you can conserve what gas you have left.

When you were a cocky 20, owning six trash bags and pride,
you didn't know he would lead you to a Ford Escort home.
Turn the car off so you can conserve what gas you have left.
It's the only way you'll see the dawn.

You didn't know he would lead you to a Ford Escort home.
Try to block out the fluorescent glow of street lamp midnight.
It's the only way you'll see the dawn—
you try not think about tomorrow.

Michael Dwayne Smith
Andanza Motel, Anaheim, California

Happy place on Earth, Disneyland's only a block up. Those 9:30
fireworks brighten shadow and ache a moment, and at least
we're not sleeping in the park. Min-wage job and a bus line and we
hold on to just what's in front of us. Spaghetti-in-a-can dinner.

Days can be hard, a kind of selective truth maybe. Like it's true
most of the kittens born in the blue trash bin by number nineteen
won't survive. At least this family's got fighting chances.

Beat the odds to get a room here. Was tossed out of one last week
on account of Nicky's slugfests (misses her mom, God rest). Fate
deals our hand, but my three ragged little bandits and one stray
stay all together behind grins or walls or parking lots.

At sundown, I draw the nicotine curtains, dull the failure of light.
Some flies will have died and baked on the sill. Our surviving
tabby stalks others, buzzing half-alive against the yellow glass—

I lay on the crowded mattress, where sleep overtakes me, dim stars
grimacing at the window. I lay down in wonder, in awe of nothing.

Donna Hilbert
1942 Snapshot of my Father

He could be my child,
this boy at seventeen,
centered in front of a palm tree
in the parkway
of his sister's yard.
This motherless kid,

in a borrowed sports coat
and slacks that fold
too deeply over his shoes.
His curly hair is combed back.
His lips part in an almost grin.

I know the history of this picture:
how he came to California to find work.
How he dug ditches, riveted metal,
picked fruit,
returned to Oklahoma to marry his girl
before he turned eighteen. Nothing

to remark about, given the war.
And I know the life that followed:
the guns hidden in chimneys, bruises
under scarves, how the half-smile
concealed a boozy rage. Still,

it moves me:
how he glistens in this picture,
the deep crease of his slacks,
his boyish curls.

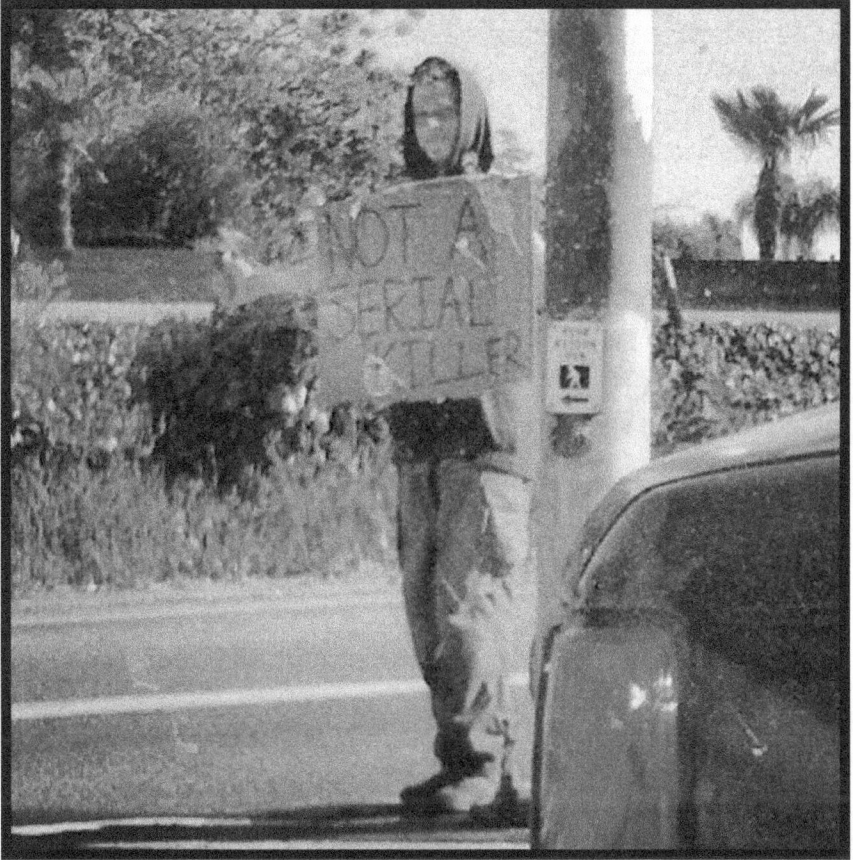

Rain Sheiman
Good to Know

Forrest Valdiviez
Chicago's World

At the Greyhound station in Seattle, I met a man from Chicago who said he was there to turn his life around. He wore Italian loafers, gold jewelry, and a Chicago White Sox jacket. He said he had been a pimp, but had been chased out of town by the cops.

"Life is hard," he said, "but I'm trying to turn my life around. All I need is some change."

I handed over a dollar and lit a cigarette. As I took my first puff, a little woman all dressed in pink walked up and asked if she could buy a cigarette.

"I'll tell you what," I said, "you can HAVE a cigarette. How's that?"

"Thanks," she said, "that's the best thing to happen to me all day."

She moved around with a jitter, like she had snorted a few lines of crank. "Why are people so messed up? I fed a woman and her kids in Tacoma and the woman stole my wallet. Can you believe that?"

Me and Chicago said we couldn't believe it. The world was a rotten place.

She said she had been on her way to Canada to visit her husband, whom she hadn't seen in five months. She was pregnant.

"I don't care about the wallet," she said. "All it had was $6. What sucks is that she took my I.D. and you can't get into Canada without I.D. So I'm stuck here."

"You need some money?" Chicago asked.

"No," she said, "I don't need money. I've got money. What I need is my I.D. You guys want to see something crazy?"

We shrugged.

There, in front of everyone in front of the bus station, she pulled out a pouch filled with jewelry.

"This watch alone is worth $1,200," she said, holding it up and making it sparkle.

Chicago's eyes lit up.

"In that case, why don't you help a brother out?" he said. "All I need is $3. You have a beautiful soul, I can tell. You have inner beauty. The world is cold, but you aren't. I can tell. So how about $3? I'm trying to turn my life around. You can help me. I can tell."

She said he had to break a $100, but that she could help him out. Later. He told her not to forget. She went inside.

Chicago turned to me asked me what I was doing in Seattle.

I told him I was going to a friend's wedding reception.

He said he hadn't had a job in three months, but he was looking.

I said I hadn't had a job in seventh months, and I was too.

"You go to college?"

"Yeah. Journalism."

"And you can't get a job? Not even in Los Angeles with all your people?'

"Not even in L.A."

He looked at me, this man who had no job, no money, no home, no friends and said, "DAMN!"

I shrugged.

"I should give you your money back, but I'm not going to do that, 'cuz I'm trying to turn my life around," he said. "What I'm going to do is give you a tip. Never carry your money in your wallet. I don't. I keep my hundreds in my sock or shoe. You could get mugged or knifed for your money. There are desperate people here in Seattle."

I agreed and went back into the station. I had four hours to kill before my hotel room was ready. I paced the station, read a book, and chewed on Chicago's words. After a while, I went back outside for a smoke.

Chicago was gone, but the pregnant woman was there, telling her story to someone else. She was squatting upon the ground, running her fingers through her long brown hair, chain smoking. A tiny bird hopped on the ground beside her.

Small, petite, it pecked at pieces of debris on the sidewalk, then let the pieces fall out the side of its beak. She repeated her story. It pecked at debris.

Hop. Repeat. Peck. Repeat.

Repeat.

I put out my smoke and went back inside.

Kay Sundstrom
Postcards

In the motel parking lot, my brother Stephen shoots plastic arrows
at our hopper green station wagon, sleeping bags piled.
"Can we have a pool shaped like a bass guitar,"
he asks, "when we get to California?" I float shiny gum wrapper boats
in a pool of spilled diet coke, my knees barnacled
with scabs and mosquito bites.

As we drive, we count road kills,
eighteen wheelers and roadside attractions,
one a germanium red lobster named "Shanky,"
his claws bristling with spikes like a cactus. "Did you spike my drink,"
Mom's first words to Dad she tells us. "His eyes were so smiling,"
she adds laughing. When she tells us this, I always see a round cup
with an iron nail reaching upward like a wooden church spiral.

"You can drink it," Mom says pointing to a barrel cactus,
her hand slicing the air, a coffee bittern bird's wing.
"Even if you get lost, you'll never die," she says.
"You promise," Stephen asks. Seven years old eyes,
fearful rabbit eyes. The rabbits always knew
when Dad was coming for them, pressed so tight
against the mesh, their bodies checkerboards
of fur and metal. I learned not to cry. Things simply are.

Mom tapes Dad's latest postcard to the dashboard.
"Found work. This time it will work. I love you all. Come."
We have postcards from almost every state: pine flats from Idaho.
Rio Grande armadillos, New Mexico gas station with pipestem hoses.
He finds jobs, janitor, McDonald's, grocery store bagger.
But they never pay enough for him to save first and last month
even though he sleeps in his dented 65 Buick.

Some nights Mom just drives, Stephen and I spooned tight.
Smelling his neck I remember I love him even though he still cries.

Dad once worked in a diner, brought home day old cherry pie,
placemats I could draw on. When he kissed me goodnight,
I could hear jukebox songs. "Be my baby, do wah."

Even though I'm 13, I am still his baby.
Mom stoops beside me, touches my spearmint boat with a bitten nail.
"Where is this one going?" she asks.
"I don't know yet," I say watching the bilious beige door
of room 13 open, a 19-year-old girl, baby on her hip
with a dried cereal scabbed face wearing booties shaped like bunnies.
We simply watch each other, her cherry popsicle melting
turning her hand columbine pink.

Fernando Gallegos
RV

Viannah E. Duncan
Possibly Icarus

The bird, grounded,
definitely dead.
Beneath the 210 freeway overpass,
a hole under its wing
looked like the absence of a prune.

Except for the part eaten away,
it would've shluffed the dirt from its wings
and risen on the air. The broken humerus
meant it would never fly again,
alive or not.

Touch it? Move it? Bury it?
never crossed my mind
but photographing it seemed
a possibility.
Did the bird know something?

Perhaps if I preserved it—even just a picture
snared in time—I could have it explain.
Then I dismissed the morbid idea, gilded cage or no.
Instead, my eyes caught the sky
and I dreamed of Daedelus.

Odilia Galván Rodríguez
Anywhere USA
Sin Casa/Homeless Series

1
Noche
my new name is Night
i live out of sight~buried
in these streets paved gold

2
Tlazolteotl
my name's Trash Eater
Icky to the likes of you
i eat all your sins

3
River
you people block me
i fight back cutting   designs
red lines in my smooth stone

4
The Shelter
church folks
ask me if I
have accepted Jesus
as my own personal savior
I'm so tired of this and
mumble - yes, hasn't everyone?
Jesus stares from his cross
rolls his brown eyes
he knows

5
Baby at 15
what kind
of a child would
you have turned out   to be
had you been allowed   to give birth
back then

6
I wasn't born, I was hatched
me llamo Noche
naci de plumas negras
del pecho de mi madre
mi name is Night
I was born from black feathers
from my mother's chest

7
Street Sleeping
morning
came with kicks   from
cops   who wish we would go
back to where we came from   which is
right here

8
Left to the Elements
last time
i forgot to
take my meds   we were lost
wind ate my child   fire won't give
him back

9
When Opportunity Quits Knocking
the slamming of doors
on my best face   crushed my mind
rusted the hinges

10
The Ripper
when i
was inside my moms
sleeping in the dark a
man put a knife to our neck, threw
her down
he said
if you scream i'll
kill you and that yummy
baby in here - so he ripped her
clothes off
by the
side of the IC
train tracks he hated us
for hours ~ made me bleed out our
body

11
Uncertain Futures
you walk past my hand
empty ~ my lonely corner
one paycheck away

LeAnne Hunt
Trailer Park Mazes Have No Exits

You entered the trailer park with a swell under your skirt.
The quick ceremony under your daddy's watchful eye
and your momma's averted face was the welcome mat
you stepped across to the threshold of slamming screen doors,
the sharp retort of a backhand across a woman's face, the endless
wailing of a dirty, runny-nosed toddler,
and the leaning towers of stacked beer cans, monuments
to what one night in the backseat of a car can crush.

Crickets sing promises at dusk when the light turns blue and lonely
and the dust settles, worn out from the heat, but in morning stale
cigarette smoke trails the walls and carpet like ants searching
for sugar. Honey catches more flies than vinegar, but vinegar
cleans. Honey coats their fragile wings, holds them down
until they tire of the struggle,
and embalms them in the heaviness of summer.

Trailer parks only have one road in; no one ever really leaves.
The pounding of rain on the aluminum siding always beats
in the inner ear, and the taste of rice and beans lingers
on the tongue like a fading bruise on skin. The smell of tar
and whiskey, asphalt and diapers, sweat
and packed dirt clings like dresses
see-through thin from too many washings.

Mickie Lynn
You Stay Where You Can Afford

Later, my sister and I admitted
to the nightly fear,
cockroaches crawling
into our ears or mouths
as we slept.
They like dark places.

That apartment was inundated.
Two species skittered
across counters and carpets,
especially after the sun went down.

Itty bitty black ones rounded
slightly like matchstick heads.
The other, a half-inch long,
colored caramel.

In the middle of the night
light flicked on,
watching them scatter
across walls as we peed.

On the table, five
dead carcasses float
in an inch of red Kool-Aid.
I wondered how they crawled
up the slippery glass.

We weren't dirty people.
I had never seen a cockroach
until we moved there.
They like dark places:

drawers, cupboards, cabinets,
toasters, eight-track players.

We kept little when we moved.

I screamed when one jumped
from the shadowy recesses
of my Barbie Dream House.

Isaac Chavarría
Colonia Park Transport

Odilia Galván Rodríguez
Ponies
for Dee Dee

my first pony blue
warrior made in the USA   1957
bought in 1977 for
one-hundred dollars
a fortune to me then

Chevy with manual column shifting
no power steering   before stick
shifts were in   out again
back seat full of black top
        broken and spit
through a big hole in the floor

I'd grown up in a city of buses
the L snakes winding
tunneling through the town
no reason to drive cars
Chicago Transit Authority
        for getting   around

Moms came from Texas
couldn't part with hers
so many old and broken down
kept them sitting in the railroad yard
behind the Projects where we lived

our prairie
though kids not allowed
because of hoboes passing through
we'd disobey   make those cars forts
our motto   you can't hurt steel

holes in floors are nothing new
but a pony needs to be reliable
no matter what
even if people point
laugh at its looks

who cares   you know
theirs is probably no better
an old beater brought back to life
like those old mustangs waiting
in the junk yard   other '57s

those one-eyed fords of our youth
dappled with rust   painted primer gray
mufflers held up
by duct tape and bailing wire
doors and trunks tied shut with climber's rope

Indian cars   part of our story
we're nations
proud of our ponies
these vehicles that give us hope

Nancy Scott
The Inheritance

Her hair braided with yellow extensions, Pauline says,
I've been feeling poorly. She has an umbrella
in her chest and blood clots in her legs.
Surrounded by a sea of black plastic bags, she's ready

to move. She needs a larger apartment for herself,
her disabled daughter, a granddaughter and two kids

on welfare, her oldest son who's no longer *incompensated.*
Out of prison? I ask and she nods, and another son

who's run off, she doesn't know where, but he'll be home
any day now. Her youngest won't be coming.

Two months ago he passed, an attack of sickle-cell
the emergency room doctor missed.

How many bedrooms can I get? Pauline asks.
Three bedrooms, I say, and she doesn't dispute this.

She rummages around in a ripped vinyl purse,
hands me a wad of stained documents: award letters,

birth certificates, social security cards.
What will happen to my family if...

Anyone 18 or older can keep the rental subsidy, I say.
This is the first time I've seen Pauline smile.

Nancy Lynée Woo
Invocation of Sandini* During an Era of Apartment Hunting
after Brendan Constantine

O French-fried mornings
      O cracked cement, black spittle-spot sidewalk
          O friendly cockroach
             O cigarette butt unanchored
                O condom, mystery

I supplicate to your window smells—
      bacon, fried chicken, barbecue
I kneel to your helicopter gaze
      your ice cream truck jingles
         black bar doorways
      O second story ceiling fans, keep me cool
tamale lady, keep me hungry

      O mariachi Mondays (and Tuesdays
         and Wednesdays,   Thursdays,   Fridays,
      especially Saturdays and Sundays)
O boombox bicyclists, bobbing head, grin dreadlocked
         Snoop Dogg take me back to the '90s

Sandini thank you!
      For your glorious dinge
         your alleyway kickball, rare parkscapes
            graffiti fences, yellowing grass

Thank you for our recycling bins
      bike lanes, night clubs, coffee shops
and please bless us
         with a 2-bedroom apartment in the yellow
            or pink crime range
         a clean refrigerator, parking space(s)
            and on-site laundry

O please
let there be laundry
and parking

O divine Sandini!

O heat vent kittens!
O menacing boys!
O dog poop!
O litter!

Let us not wither
despair
be robbed
stabbed
stalked
too desperate

I will learn how to parallel park, I promise
and nod to the bearded man on the street,
more when I have leftovers

O candy wrapper side yards
O bright lights curbside
O grime
O grit
O city

Come, envelope me in your hard
knowing, talk to me here
let me wander & sit
& cough with you
daylong

*a black-winged goddess of especially dingy cities (that the author
made up)

Sharon Elliott
Homeless

woman with kids

on the edge
you have to know
how not to be poor
and they don't teach that in school

frozen bone
inaccessible marrow
endless
unfulfillable expectations
reflections in department store windows

living on the streets
Nintendo is
an expletive
shaming kids
who ain't got one

free food is undernourishing
makes a roly poly statement
of fat and flesh
it's hard to receive benefits
or apply for a job
without an address
and then
rent isn't really covered
bills
clothes
school supplies
let alone food

day is a waking burden
long hot cement
beneath aching feet
struggles to find a doorway
an alley
to take a piss
later
searching for one
that doesn't smell like piss
to rest in
sleepy time a nightmare

washing hungry little faces
in gas station bathrooms
that no longer exist
key or no key
raggedy clothes
smelling
like years of no detergent

the hum and roll
of a dryer in a warm laundry room
are dreams fading into mist
cold apple juice from a fridge
grilled-cheese sandwich
become legends
bare feet
in green grass
not a choice anymore
but a requiem

Karla Cordero
Home is where the heart grows cold

The sun hates to visit here.
It pushes itself through broken mini blinds
bringing light to a room god probably doesn't know exists.

I notice the spider on the ceiling corner finally died from a night terror,
Mother says, *It must have dreamt about living here forever.*

She lifts her body off ground,
her bones beg for mattress.
She ignores pain, smiles, tells me,
The homeless have it worse than we do.
Concrete floors are no place for dreaming.

My stomach interrupts our morning conversation.
A rude organ knocking on my ribcage.
I pour pennies out the pickle jar.
Mother boils a box of nails on stove.
She says, *Iron's good for the heart.*

I tell her,
At least the homeless can beg.

Donna Hilbert
Madill
for my father

At the dog races in Tijuana
you waited all day to bet on Madill,
dog named the same as the Oklahoma
town you were born in. Madill—
done in before he rounded the track.

Six years dead, you're coming back to me,
in Reseda, September, the house on Canby,
laying brick around the flowerbed,
beer cans gleam from the fence top,
sweat beads glister your back.

I imagine it was hot like this,
your mama barely two weeks dead,
the day you and Buddy sat on the fence,
feet tucked under the wooden slats,
Pa's cow a target for your Bowie knife,

dreaming of another life, you let the handle fly.

Karlee A. Tittle Cuff
Junkyard Dog

David S. Pointer

soup plate bones
hungry dog turns away
his master does not

Nancy Scott
Lost Boy of Sudan

As soldiers level their rifles to fire,
five-year-old Daniel drops the rope
and slips into the Gilo River.
After miles of dry grass and African sun
how quenching the water will be.
But no friendly river is in this story.
Someone forgot the clock
that belongs in the crocodile's belly,
one ticking so loudly, Daniel must swim
to the other shore for safety.

Here time is shaped by the Baobab,
its root-like branches snarling the sky.
Kick, feral child, while the second-hand
floats free of the vulture's wing.

Sarah Thursday
Murrieta

When you rise early from your wide bed
pull on your long pants, brush your porcelain teeth,
do you also decide to fill your mouth with pebbles
stuff them into your cheeks for stoning small children?

When you gather the keys to your reliable car,
drink your coffee, eat your toast and eggs,
do you then grab your territorial pissing sign,
join others pushing buses full of babies off the road?

When you kiss your mop-haired children goodnight,
stroke their cool foreheads, wish them quiet dreams,
do you tell them of slashing plastic jugs of water,
pouring it out into sand like a narrow-eyed bully?

When you brush off the knees of your own fallen children,
teach them to be fair and kind, grow up strong,
do you tell them how you dream of kicking the skins
of skinny brown legs, barely able to stand?

*On July 2, 2014, dozens of protesters in Murrieta, CA, blocked 3
buses of refugee women and children from being processed in their
facilities. In 2012, the humanitarian group No More Deaths
documented border patrol officers kicking, slashing, and pouring out
jugs of water left for desert crossers.*

Ricki Mandeville
because...

of *no*
    I am tired
        I am hungry
            no one gives a damn

there is nowhere to sleep
    you think I will spend it on booze
        I am *tired poor huddled*
            I am *wretched* I am *refuse*

my shoes have holes, my socks
    touch the sidewalks
        there is never enough
            the day is too long

the statue is a liar
    they always look away
        I am invisible
            I hurt

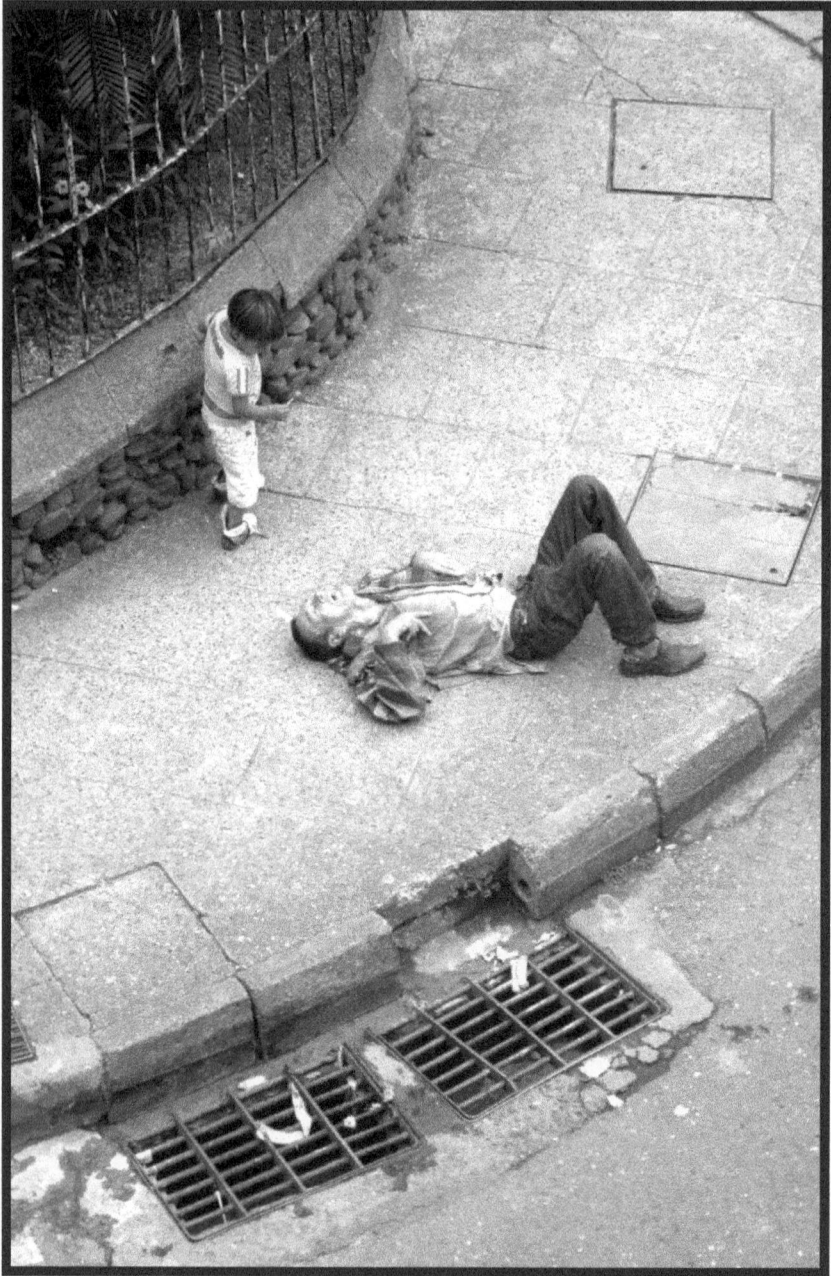

Brian Coe
Sucker

Alejandro Duarte
I Have Been, part 5

Standing at the foot of night burning
canisters of shadow from sky I am
the keeper of fires blue like water

hot & cleansing, ward thieves away
stars who steal our dreams & have
when you sleep, through windows

reach with spiraling tendrils of air
like goddamned wind entering
our orifices, leaving colored trails

of infrared & ultraviolet biting
by their tiny feet they find us.
Think about it & I want a fine red

wine too, by this fire's light. Keep me
sky warm & I will wash their crawling

from devouring you, like me. It's dawn
& I'm painful clean, take me beneath
any park or bridge with a clear spot

grass or dirt pretending to be
dark so I can sleep & hide.

Part Three: Money

Thomas R. Thomas
hopeless

shuffle stilted walk
you drift through
we invisible you

breasts bounce
in ill fitting
castoff clothes

blank stare
even you can't
stand the smell

sanity gone
stopped being
a woman

too long
to remember
stopped being

human
stopped
being

Susan Lefler
Bullet Points for a Winter Storm

Code Purple:
- implemented when temperature drops below 20 degrees
- the homeless invited to stay at churches, no questions asked.
- churches to provide, the volunteers, the food
- local law enforcement prepared to be involved
- this county has no such plan in place

Code—trunk of a tree, tablet of wood covered with wax for writing on, systematic statement of a body of law, system of principles or rules, system of words or symbols arbitrarily used to represent words, protocol following an event, the word hospitals use when someone's heart has stopped.

Purple—the color of emperors and kings, of Tyrian dye from the mucus of a tiny snail, stoles and altar hangings during Lent, amethysts and eggplants, plums, fuchsia blossoms, the grapes of cabernet, purple hearts for valor, purple prose marked by profanity, the color of a bruise, the purple tint the skin takes on when you sleep beneath a highway bridge at night and the temperature drops.

Nancy Lynée Woo
The Crash

He looks down the barrel of the gun like he's looking down the ass of a stripper like he's looking down the throat of his daughter like he's looking down the bottom of a shot glass like he's looking down the blouse of his wife flirting with another man like he's looking down the engine of his favorite 1967 cobalt blue Mustang like he's looking down the paperwork of the IRS sweeping him clean like he's looking down at the cement from a twelve-story building like he's looking down into the cavernous hole of his mother's womb. "Daddy." He spins from the chair, hits the ground, sees tiny claws outlined in the dust of the blow. "Daddy," the bird caws. His empire burning to ash in the beak. Bankers clamor out of the building, ties on fire, chased by janitors who scream they saw it coming and where do we go now. Powder on his skin. Sleeping in the car from now on. Asphalt suits, clinking glasses, alarm in the building, evacuate, evacuate. The tiny bird shines iridescent as it dances and squawks, "You could have seen it coming." The man lies there on the motel carpet, a roach twirling pirouettes. From afar, sirens blare and a woman outside shouts, "Ain't you never comin' back here, boy!" I'm never coming back, the gun whispers. Barrel-heavy lids struggle to close. Cat food stinks on the street and he remembers a coloring book his mother gave him. I can't feed you, he says to the bird. The water drains from his eyes as the drip of the faucet winks. I'll be eating salmon from cans, he thinks, and falls into sleep. In a dream, he stares down the barrel of the gun like an African hunter staring down the jaws of a crocodile, one red eye twitching. The bones crackle as they split. "Daddy." His claw clenches the neck of that bird. Please shut up, he says as she grows into a woman from ruins.

Sadie Shorr-Parks
Greys, Counted Carefully

I borrowed from my mother.
A cinder-block bookcase, chicken bone soup

I can't help but return to our cement-floors in Pittsburgh.
Shallow pools of grey
I'm silently taking stock.

She taught me the art of the barter, the beginning, but not all of it.
A tangle of jewelry tossed in a bag.

A row of rusted days. Blank.
Need is the only thing that can really change a person.

My mom wanted to carve her body baroque.
The bravest thing I am is round.

Pittsburgh, I have borrowed without returning:

A cinder block nativity scene,
A place to stack small books.

What do you have left to barter with?
My mom stacks her folded cotton shirts;

I want everything I do to be like that.

She can fold me into soft cotton and I try to be brave and round.
I love her. She showed me the art in my cluster of scraps.

Rococo bodies carved my mother.
Really, this is the only thing.

And that some place, where empty equals vast,
She tried to crawl out of the cavity of the steel mill.

Don Kingfisher Campbell
Animals

On a blustery day
a baseball cap flies
to the sidewalk off
tousled salty hair
And I pick up
that hat and hand
it back to the man
who asks for change
I tell him yes
because he's a Mariner
fan and he looks
puzzled so I point
To the blue trident
stitched onto canvas
above his lined brow
—he's still bewildered
I dump all my coins
into his weathered palm,
walk inside for snacks and
glance when I leave
He's lying on the grass
by the curb and I
wonder where he'll sleep
tonight as I hug my life
All I can think of
as I drive away—
I've only chosen twice
to snooze under stars
And he's a windswept mouse
with an unasked history
while I'm a happy hamster
pampered by a career cage

Daniel McGinn
November

This week we arrived at a work-comp settlement,
or settled for what we are going to get;
we're getting one third of one year's income.
I juiced greens, did the dishes, gimped around the house
and accepted what I cannot change. I accept what this is.
I'd grown miserable in the position I was in.
I'm below the poverty line now, but I'm happier.

A coyote walked down the middle of our street
in the middle of the day, only yesterday.
My dog started to bark-whine
and I went to see what was wrong.
There was nothing but a window screen
separating my dog and a coyote.
The coyote looked well fed.
It stood in our front yard and sniffed the air.
I picked my dog up; we looked out the window together.
The coyote appeared to be smiling
as it turned and walked away.

This afternoon, after I signed the settlement papers,
Lori retired to the bedroom to huddle under blankets.
She stayed under most of the day,
only getting up once or twice
to tell me that she did not want to live,
because life isn't fair.
She pointed out that the two of us
would be driving used cars into our graves.

Lori got out of bed last night,
right after the sun went down.
We stood in the front yard and looked at the full moon.

It was huge.
It feels like fall, I said.
Yeah, she said, *but it looks a little off around the edges.*
I accepted that and went back into the house.

Last night, as soon as I fell asleep, I was two inches tall.
I watched myself walk on a six-by-twenty-foot conveyor.
This conveyor belt led to the paper grinder.
The grinder was rumbling but there was no paper on the belt.
I was alone in the recycling plant.
I was certain I had forgotten something.
My equipment was up and running.
I knew the crew should be around here somewhere.
Something was wrong. Was it something I did,
or something I didn't do?
I knew I was supposed to be somewhere
doing something. I kept on walking the conveyor.
Was I supposed to be at the courthouse?
Then, suddenly, I wasn't on a conveyor at all,
I was in my maintenance cage
wiping grease from my hand tools.
My boss started yelling at me like I was his dog,
Stay! You stay!
I looked at my toolbox as I answered him,
I can't stay; I have to go to court.
Then he asked, in anger, *When are you going to wake up?*

Tonight I'm sitting at the back porch, listening to the rain.
Lori is angry at me because I don't fight back.
I'm not angry.
I moved on and the fight moved behind me;
it's cold out here and I can't see the moon.

Dr. Ernest Williamson III
Social Misery

Malke Singer
Telephone Talk

in Oakland I can hear
through the window
my son's birth mother opens
all the way in Baton Rouge
long telephone talk
about racism in America

she is black and I am white
she's off the street found a little trailer
on Waffle House wages with good neighbors
no drugs around she's proud
of her good news I kvell over her success

although her rheumatoid arthritis is flared up
for now she sees no crisis on the horizon
just so good to be home a bedroom for her
and one for my son's brother   we celebrate it

with a long heart to heart cell phone
talk for once the reception is crystal clear

Don Kingfisher Campbell
Hood Mouse

you strip down to your boxer shorts
when you get that rare opportunity
to swim in somebody's pool
(and you shiver like a rat
when you get out because
you didn't bring a towel)
you say your ears bleed sometimes
but you don't have an earache
—no need to go to the doctor—it goes away
you don't like the taste
of fat free buttermilk pancakes
with 48% vegetable spread
and Country Rich Lite syrup
(that's what happens
when you stay over
at your sister's friend's apartment)
you brag you have a friend
who works with computers—
selling for just $300—
after stealing them first
(and you inquire with interested
eyes as to how much I
paid for my computer)
you complain that the new project
you've moved into with your six siblings
(six different fathers) is noisier
because of those nightly gun shots
your two bedroom government subsidized
apartment lacks a dining table,
a sofa, but has plenty of beds
you get bored, you close your eyes,
turn to your side to sleep on the floor

while the family you're visiting
watches anything on PBS or black and white
your idea of reading in the fourth grade
is a Dr. Seuss book, preferably
an Early Reader edition
and this is all true, your
sometimes-at-home mom takes Zoloft
and you're not even a teenager yet

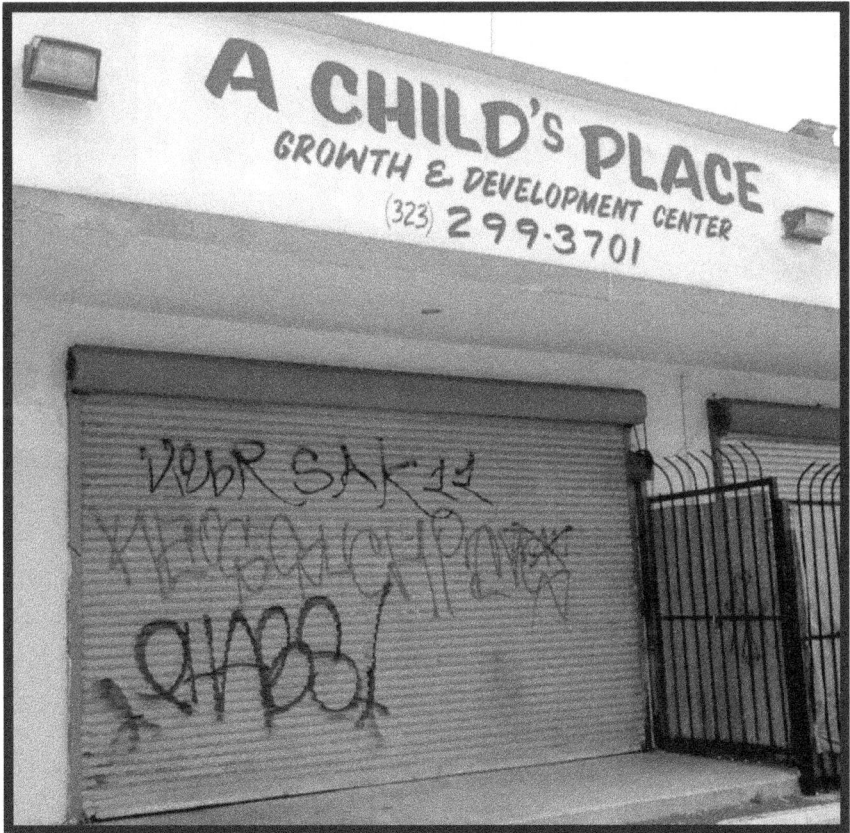

Karlee A. Tittle Cuff
A Child's Place

Matt Peters
Hunters and Gatherers

Reese circles the La Rue House Youth Shelter, staying hidden behind the wall that surrounds the parking lot. It is past dinner, but he hopes to pick-up some leftovers, and maybe a safe place to sleep for the night.

Reese is only twenty years old, but red blotches stain his face, ears and neck. And crow's-feet already walk at the corners of his eyes. The Florida sun eases the cruelty of winter, but years of exposure to even pleasant conditions leave their mark. Reese's hair stands off his scalp and is too thick and clumped and ragged to pass as simply his style. It's just unkempt and unwashed. The only time he combs it is when it blocks his vision or pokes him in the eyes, and then he simply paws it back over his head.

Jernell and Jernell's girlfriend, Sin, follow Reese closely. Jernell's hair is tapered short against his scalp, and his clothes are still clean. He carries an overstuffed backpack and pulls Sin along by the hand. She is thin with dark hair, has dark rings under her eyes and her cheeks are hollow.

Reese hops up on some discarded pallets that are stacked next to the wall and looks over. Jernell does the same and they scout out the shelter's parking lot and main entrance.

Ms. Gloria's car is in the lot, and Reese figures chances are good for a real meal. He elbows Jernell and points to a blonde girl on the front steps of the shelter. He recognizes her from earlier visits to the shelter: Tonya, the girl with a car who would never give him a ride anywhere.

Tonya pounds on the glass door of the shelter and Ms. Gloria looks up from the In-Take desk. Tonya swings her purse high in the air, showing it to Ms. Gloria. "I've got it right here," Tonya yells at the door. The purse sparkles in the overhead light.

Ms. Gloria's voice crackles through the intercom speaker and echoes through the parking lot. "You want to deposit it now?"

"No," Tonya yells. "But I've got it, so you can stop looking through my stuff and just give it to me."

"We're packing it as fast as we can," Ms. Gloria says and goes back to her work.

Tonya kicks the door and yells, "If I'm discharged, then you can stop writing notes about me."

"If you don't stop," Ms. Gloria says, "you'll have to leave the property."

Tonya stomps her foot and yells, "I'm not leaving until you give me my shit."

"Then settle down, or I'll call the police and have you charged with trespassing," Ms. Gloria says. "Then you'll never be able to come back."

"I'm never coming back anyway," Tonya yells and puffs her body up. She's about to kick the door again but stops and sets her purse on top of the trash can.

Back behind the wall, Reese smiles at the purse, dimples appearing in his cheeks. She's got money. If he can get some of it, he can buy a combo meal at Burger King or get some beer and weed, or maybe even get a room for the night. "No problem," he tells Jernell. "Staff's already busy with her. They'll give us something just to get rid of us."

Jernell nods, learning.

"We'll be right back," Reese tells Sin and pulls himself over the wall.

Jernell sets down his backpack and kisses Sin. "We'll be right back."

"Don't fuck up," she tells him as he climbs over the wall.

Reese scans the parking lot as they cross to the shelter's door, but nobody is walking around, and no one's sitting in any of the cars. They both glace at Tonya as they approach the front door. Her arms are folded across her knees, and her face is buried in them; she's no threat.

The boys smile and wave for the security camera, but Ms. Gloria doesn't respond, so Reese knocks on the door.

Ms. Gloria jolts in surprise, then slouches like she's tired. They smile and wave at her. "Hello, Reese. Hello, Jernell," she greets them through the intercom. "What do you need?"

"We don't have any money for the Coalition," Reese says, using the name of the most inexpensive adult shelter to make them seem more in need. "And we used up our free nights at the Salvation Army," he adds before she can suggest it.

Even if he had the money, he wouldn't stay at any of the adult shelters downtown. Here at La Rue, Reese is one of the big dogs, an old-timer with power and respect. At the adult shelters, he's a puppy, easily pushed away from the food and on the losing end of every confrontation.

"Hold on," Ms. Gloria tells them and looks through a box of index cards. She pulls out two cards. "You have no overnights left."

This is no surprise to Reese, but experience has taught him to always ask for something on the random chance that he might get it. He never knows when he might catch a break, so he's always on the lookout for the next one.

Ms. Gloria adds, "You'll have to wait until your cards are up."

"When's that?" Reese asks to keep her talking.

As Ms. Gloria glances back at the cards, he scans the parking lot. Tonya is still sitting in the same spot, but now she is drying her face with her sleeves.

"Three days for Jernell," Ms. Gloria says. "A week for you."

"A week?" Reese asks and looks to Jernell, who is looking back at the wall. Reese pops him with the back of his hand.

Jernell starts and looks back at Ms. Gloria and asks, "Can we get something to eat?"

"You're supposed to come before nine," she reminds them, sounding stern.

"We didn't have any bus passes," Reese says. "We had to walk." He knows she will feed them; she never denies anyone food.

"I'll see what I can find," Ms. Gloria says and stands to leave the desk.

"What was for dinner?" Reese asks, hoping to get some real food instead of the brown bag lunches the shelter usually gives out.

"Peanut butter and jelly," Ms. Gloria answers with a smile.

"We need three," Jernell adds before Ms. Gloria can leave the desk.

Ms. Gloria looks at the security monitors by her desk. "Who's with you?" she asks.

"My girlfriend," Jernell says and glances back toward the wall.

"Who's that?" Ms. Gloria asks.

"Someone who's been trespassed," Reese answers to move things along.

Ms. Gloria shakes her head at them and leaves the office.

Reese scans the parking lot again. Nothing appears to be going on. Sin peeks over the wall, and Jernell gives her a thumbs-up. Reese steps off the curb and stands in front of Tonya. "Got a smoke for a quarter?" he asks her.

Tonya nods and digs her cigarettes out of her coat pocket. She passes him a cigarette and her lighter. He slides his hand into his pocket to get the change, but she waves him off and says, "Don't worry about it." She gives Jernell a cigarette too and takes another for herself.

Reese notices the lighter is new, still full of fuel. Tonya must have a lot of money if she has a new lighter and is giving away cigarettes. He lights Jernell's cigarette but doesn't pass him the lighter.

"What you doing out here?" Reese asks Tonya, hoping that if he's nice to her, she'll leave with them and take him somewhere in her car. No more walking. No more buses.

"I got discharged," Tonya says, sniffling short and quick to hide that she's been crying. "They're packing my stuff."

"What'd you get discharged for?" Reese asks. He squats down next to her, getting close. She might even have sex with him.

"Not giving them the money from my check," she answers.

"Where you work?" Jernell asks.

Reese smiles because Jernell has learned this trick. It's always good to know people with regular jobs and to know where they work, especially if it's someone who'll give you free food or let you shoplift while they are working.

Tonya shakes her head. "Social Security," she says.

Jernell steps away from her. "You get a crazy check?" he asks.

"I'm not crazy!" she shouts at him, making Jernell move farther away. "Don't you go thinking I'm crazy," Tonya yells. "It's those fucking doctors..."

Reese scowls at Jernell to make him behave and keep him from ruining this.

"I know. It's cool," Reese interrupts to quiet her. He slides behind her and rubs her shoulders. Crazy or not, if he can snare her, he'll have a way to get around and a safe place to get high and sleep.

"They don't understand," she tells Reese. "I need my money. Stupid staff want me to find a job and save my money. I got to take care of my car first."

Reese looks around the lot for her car. Worried now, because he doesn't remember seeing it when they came up. "Where's your car?" he asks.

"Impounded," she says. "Cause these fuckers won't let me keep it here."

"Shit," Reese says, sorry to lose the use of her car. "You got a place to go?" he asks, still hoping for a safe place to sleep and to have sex with her.

"No," she says shaking her head.

Reese strokes her back. "You'll be okay."

"How much to get your car out?" Jernell asks.

"Three-fifty."

"Damn," the boys sympathize in unison. Three hundred and fifty dollars is a fortune. Reese can't remember that last time he had even a hundred dollars.

"Forget that," Reese adds. She'll never see her car again.

"I got the money," she says, jerking her thumb over her shoulder at her shiny purse. "These fucking people won't let me use it to get my car back." She points inside at Ms. Gloria's empty desk. "They want me to deposit it."

Reese looks at the purse and can feel the money that is inside: three hundred and fifty dollars. Food. Shelter. Warmth. Safety. The money is only three feet from him.

He glances at Jernell, who is asking her, "Why won't they let you get your car?"

"They say I got to deposit the money into saving first. Then I can get it out to pay for my car," Tonya explains. "But I'm not falling for that shit. They just want it so they can keep it. I know how they work."

Reese rubs her shoulders again. He doesn't know how much money is actually in the purse, but he's got to take this break. Besides, if she leaves with him, she's going to want to spend it all on getting her car back and won't spend the money on him.

Reese glances around the parking lot. No cars are pulling in from the road or even passing by. Sin watches from the wall, but no one else is around. Ms. Gloria isn't back from the kitchen yet. He looks up at the security camera. Snatching the purse here will get him a permanent card, and he won't ever be able to come back to this shelter. But with three hundred and fifty bucks, he won't need the shelter. The three hundred and fifty bucks will be his shelter.

"It'll be all right," Reese says softly to relax her and make her feel secure before he strikes.

"These fucking staff," Tonya goes on, not even watching her purse. "They drive me crazy. They're so stupid."

If he does it, Ms. Gloria'll call the cops on him. But with three hundred and fifty bucks, the cops won't be able to find him. Nothing will be able to find him. Not the cops. Not the thugs. Not the crackheads. Not the rain. Not the cold. And not even hunger will be able to find him.

He flicks his cigarette butt into the parking lot to distract Tonya. As she watches the cherry skip across the ground, he strikes without even signaling Jernell.

Reese snatches the purse and runs for the wall. He hears Tonya scream as he runs but only looks back once he reaches the wall. Jernell steps into the parking lot but is looking around like a punk and not running. Tonya grabs Jernell, and he stumbles, pulling her off the curb. They both fall onto the ground.

Reese lands on the other side of the wall and sees Sin dash behind the back corner of the next building. He smiles. She's cool. If Jernell doesn't catch up, Reese will have sex with her tonight.

K. Andrew Turner
i cannot afford

new shoes
to fix my bike
a new car
starbucks
going out
to buy my own food
rent
a house
writing
my dreams
entertainment
education
opportunities
to give
vacations
to die
to live.

Dan Steinbacher
we are barely here

sometimes, we
follow ourselves with
excessive forced perspective.
the two in the
alley had swastikas
tattooed over their eyelids.
   punches raining sideways
fingernails full of hair and
scabbed teeth.

we were eating something orangeish
that could not possibly
have been chicken—
too many violin strings
and bits of fur.

the smell follows us
reeking like the used
condom of a locker room
that fucked a plastic refinery,
        a smell not
        false but instead
wholly chthonic.

saw a dog expire
in that alley once,
        mange sails billowing their last
        while fleas jumped ship.
we have learned to look empty while walking.
diagonals branch from
        terrifyingly fast asphalt circles
        to access randomized gentrification.

the sunset factory was built
      downwind from us on purpose.
      it might breathe particulate into the air,
but you ain't never seen
      a more glowing evening show— .
      impossible purple tinges and
smelted gold light pouring onto
the sunken fetal alcohol faces,
bureaucracy ravaged necks.

thank you liquified dinosaurs.
thank you concrete riverbed.
thank you circling helicopter searchlight
thank you impossibly huge freighters
thank you gunshot lullabye
thank you 500 million
dollar glass and chrome
monolith courthouse
watching over an
unpaved parking lot
across the street.

there are bones
buried everywhere here.
at the witching hour
      the sky gets as dark
      as a neon pumpkin
but no darker.
our unofficial drink is
the abandoned couch.

what does the beach
long for; what is
the hill signaling to us?

Dr. Ernest Williamson III
Regardless of What You Face

Joe Gardner
Toilet Paper Epiphany

Two rolls of toilet paper
Hidden up each pant leg
Trying to walk normal
Clock out from work
Don't want anyone to know my shame
Work forty plus
Hours a week
And I still can't
Afford to
Wipe my own ass

Alexis Rueal
What Mamma Had to Do

They called her "whore,"
but Mamma did what Mamma had to do.
I saw the King James' version of a holier-than-thou attitude
from other women on the street,
watched them throw out their judgment like a hand grenade,
stand back and pray the shrapnel peel the hide from Mamma's back.

When there were no more plasma bank paychecks,
no more jewelry to pawn,
when she had to fill beer-bottle size holes in my Daddy's paychecks,
Mamma turned to the only currency she had left.

Her friends:
rent money friends,
school fee friends,
new shoes and winter coat friends,
utility bill and Christmas gift friends,
grocery friends.

I knew all Mamma's friends—
knew who I would see as I made my way up the sidewalk after school:
Daddy, three days at the Moose; his boss sitting on the back porch.
Five days out, he's nursing a coffee at the kitchen table.
A full week, Daddy's boss heading out the back door,
patting me on the head—"How ya doin', kid?"

I smiled in return. Mamma taught me to always be polite.

Entering the house and Mamma,
racing utility companies to the bank,
sending me to the grocery store for roast beef after
a week's worth of beans, cornbread, shit-on-a-shingle.

Cleaning our plates of every morsel in the kitchen,
Mamma cleaning the hate from her body
in the bathroom.
End of shift.

Woman worked every damn day.
I saw it.
Working to keep us fed, keep a roof over our heads.
Working hard to swallow her last bit of pride
as she borrowed money from my Dairy Queen tip jar.
Heard her work another man into her body in the middle of the night
while my Daddy was at the bar working a bottle
of Jack Daniels down his throat.

Mamma did what Mamma had to do;
for twenty years, I have known what my childhood cost.

I.B. Rad
God Helps Those...

While promoting cuts
for social programs,
politicians cite,
"God helps those
who help themselves"
as if it were
biblical stricture;
yet, their actions,
"speaking louder than words,"
pantomime another meaning,
"God helps those
 who help themselves [to everything]."

Marc Humpert
Faith

Mickie Lynn
Clean Water for Africa

The jug on my head
Carries death to my children
But we are thirsty

Gale Acuff
Solid Gold

After Sunday School today Miss Hooker
held me back from being free and walking
home to ask me if I've gotten saved yet,
which I haven't but at least I didn't
lie to her by saying yes, that would be
like lying to God's face, if He has one,
I should ask Miss Hooker if. So I said
No ma'am and gave her that look my puppy
gave me when he peed on my bedroom rug
and it worked, no one got hurt after that
mistake, *mercy* I guess it's called, I'm just
10 and don't know much of anything but
if I did I wonder would I throw it
around the way some people do, Preacher
Dewberry for one, and Miss Hooker, too,
when she's really got a hold of something?
Today in Sunday School it was sin, not
just any old sin but *idolatry*
is what it's called, it's there in the Bible

somewhere, the Israelites were keen on it
after Moses went up on Mount Sinai
and didn't come down for quite a spell so
they lost their faith but tried to get it back
by making a golden calf, solid gold
it was, too, Miss Hooker says, and if I
could travel back in time I'd go back then
and fetch it to right-now for her and then
maybe she'd fall in love with me and sin
is something that we'd work out together,
mine I mean, I'm sure Miss Hooker never
falls, so that when we die we'll be as one

forever up in Heaven, Miss Hooker
helping me down here. I'll melt the calf down
and sell the gold for money and put it
in the bank and Miss Hooker can retire
and I'll never have to work, we'll just make
babies when I learn how. *That* should save me.

Terry Wolverton
The Secret of Money

My mother hid money from my stepfather, whom she deemed spendthrift. She'd lie about the total in their account. Kept a wad of twenties stashed in a compartment of an old purse at the back of her closet.

I've given up balancing my checkbook. I maintain a fuzzy notion of what's in the bank, but can no longer provide a precise figure. This began last winter when I had no work.

My friend J. received an inheritance when her uncle died last year. She made extensive renovations to her home, but refuses to reveal the amount of the bequest.

Everyone is ashamed to have too much or too little—the ones who buy diamonds for their dogs and those who pick through garbage for a morsel of food.

As a child, I filched coins from the top of my parents' dresser. The splatter from my stepfather's pockets. If he ever noticed the diminished pool of silver, he never said.

My friend D. spends much of her free time in pursuit of sales and discounts. She'll invest hours of time to save a few dollars. I've seen her buy and return a pair of shoes three and four times as they are progressively discounted, until she gets the rock-bottom price.

My friend M. who works in finance, who brokers multi-million dollar deals, is predicting a market crash within the year. She's quietly advising all her friends to convert their assets to cash.

Everyone is afraid—the ones who worry that their portfolios will tank and those who harbor fears of ending up pushing a shopping cart beneath the freeway overpass.

My friend W. was born into considerable wealth. She tells me she's never ridden a subway in New York. When in Manhattan, she goes everywhere by limousine.

Several of my friends work in cash businesses—hairdressers, manicurists, masseuses, sex workers. They do not report their full income to the IRS. Before expressing outrage, remember, sixty percent of U.S. corporations pay no taxes.

Yesterday a man stopped me on the street, "Do you got a little sumpin' for a homeless brother?" I fished a dollar from my wallet. "I like that hair," he told me. "That must be a Beverly Hills haircut." "I'm not a Beverly Hills kind of girl," I told him. Only afterward did I remember that my hair cutter does in fact work in Beverly Hills.

Everyone feels aggrieved—the ones taxed at the rate of 35% and the 14% of Americans who live below the poverty line.

One picked strawberries at age nine to support her family.
One has a butler.
One was never given enough to eat when she was young.
One is retiring in his forties.
One borrows $500 to buy a car.
One has holes in her clothes.
One spends $400 on a pair of shoes.
One owns four homes.
One walked away from the top job at a film studio.
One goes to work in a private jet.
One puts off going to the dentist.
One died at County Hospital.
One works for $10 an hour.
One's father cut off her inheritance.

We are all alone with our secrets of money.

Earlier this year I had no work. I lived on what I'd saved until that was gone. Then I lived on credit cards. I was afraid I would lose my home. It was at this time I began experiencing shortness of breath.

Nancy Scott
Life after Welfare Reform

The waiting room is jammed with chairs. Adults sit stone-faced,
clutch rumpled envelopes filled with birth certificates, social
security cards, alien registrations—their poverty passports.
They stare at outdated flyers, missed opportunities pinned
to dirty walls, in English and Spanish, as if those
who can't read will somehow comprehend.

Children sit cross-legged on the floor, leaf through tattered
magazines, eyes on glossy ads for iPods and muscle cars.
The entrance door opens and shuts, blurts drafts of cold air.
Chorus of coughs. A tired child whimpers.
Marisol shoves her shopping bags closer to her feet.

At welfare, Marisol signs in to be certified, fumbles with
paystubs, receipts, prays food stamps won't be cut any more.
At WIC, her six-month-old son and three-year-old twins
are measured and weighed, so she can claim formula,
orange juice, cereal, peanut butter, hardly enough
to float her from paycheck to paycheck.

Summoned for eviction, she cowers outside the courtroom,
listens to words she doesn't understand. Two *abogados* arguing—
one from the landlord, one from Legal Aid.
When she gets to the front of the line for kids' winter coats,
the Salvation Army's got nothing left.

At the free clinic, Marisol crosses her fingers deep in her pockets,
waits for test results of her viral load, unwanted pregnancy,
X-rays for bruised ribs. The doctor reassures her
with proper care and medication, but she already owes
last month's rent, she got a shut-off notice from public service,
and the twins are sharing one winter coat.

Loaded with bags of potluck donations, she takes three buses
to get home where her ten-year-old son cracks the back of roaches
and keeps them in jars. After early Mass, she'll walk
the children to daycare, check the clock in the corner *bodega*,
then catch a taxi so she'll get to work on time
or an angry boss will find someone else to stuff envelopes.

Karen Boissonneault-Gauthier
We Wait

Suzanne Allen
Keep Them All

When you wait tables or teach, you don't quit
One job for another. You keep them both,
Keep them all because you need the money.

You skip a lot of meals because you're broke
Or busy. You eat a lot of fast food and feel guilty
When you wait tables or teach. You don't quit

Believing it will get better. You don't quit
Drinking either. You drink and save up bottles,
Keep them all because you need the money.

And you say you do it for the environment—
All that saving, reusing—you do it with people too.
When you wait tables or teach, you don't quit

Stockpiling lovers who ask nothing of you,
Lovers you never leave and you never ask to stay.
Keep them all because you need the money.

Let them buy you dinner. Meet them for lunch.
Have sex. Keep living. Keep believing that
When you wait tables or teach, you don't quit.
Keep them all because you need the money.

Nancy Lynée Woo
21st Century Sisyphus

You're heavy

mutton

flattened

by that boulder
          again

this time, weighing two grand
you must push it up
and out of the auto shop

Just as you've pushed before
the maxed out credit card
high interest on the maxed out
credit card, student loans
parking tickets
late fees for parking tickets
one boulder
          after the
                    other

And you keep pushing it   all
     up
          that
                    blasted
                              hill

Only to have it fall
back down
again

under the weight
of part-time employment
minimum wage scraps
unpaid internships
doing more for less
getting less for more

Sweating out the   school supplies
                                doctor visits
                                phone plans
                                water
                                lights
                                garbage
                                food
                                rent
                                fuel
                                to make it to the top
                                              again
Swallowing this fate
                    for eternity

As some punishing god   somewhere
        laughs

gloating, "You should have worked
                                       harder."

Part Four: Tribe

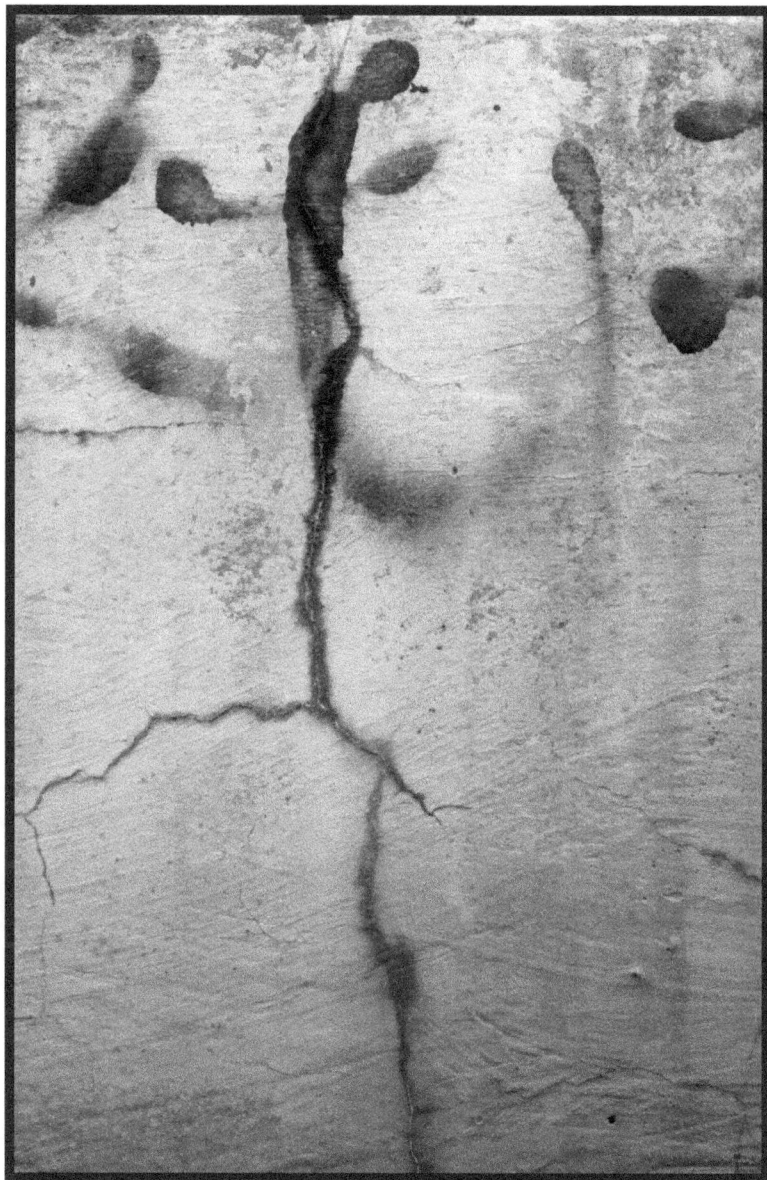

Susan Lefler
Church of the Advocate

We have come in and down to the big hall
under the old brick church. The service
begins with what you have—your name,
the thing no one can take from you.

One by one names fill the air, spoken in every register,
they build into a litany. No stories told, no reputations
made or lost. I take up the chalice and a plastic tray
of paper cups half-filled with grape juice.

I follow the priest who offers broken bread.
Each face I come to is a threshold space,
eyes clear, or wandering, or vague; hands
workworn or manicured, gnarled or tattooed.

I say the ancient words of hope and wholeness,
salve, the cup of life poured out for us,
poured into us. Tears rise in my throat
and choke me. I know nothing of each person,

only that they've come to call this their address
on Sunday afternoon, knowing we bring nothing
here except the only things we have for sure,
our hunger and our name.

Marco A. Vasquez
Hiding The Evidence

Chris chewed with his mouth open. He had big, chapped lips and hair that must have been the color of his father's. Mamá would baby-sit him and feed us sandwiches and Fritos like in commercials. Mamá spread mayonnaise and mustard on mine, neatly—right along the edge of the dark crust. She piled his on so it leaked out of the sides, and onto his hands and cheeks. His mom was always working, and dated on weekends, and beat him regularly because she was always working and had to date.

On the day after Chris' birthday, I stole his X-wing fighter just after we'd finished crookedly applying all of the decals. That night I heard his mom yelling at him. Not finding this unusual, I went outside to hear him cry and heard his mom asking him to look for his X-wing, then smacked him. With every smack, Chris' screams grew louder. This frightened me—thinking that she might find out that I took it and inflict on me the same abuse. I went and retrieved the plastic star-fighter from behind the trash cans and threw it on the roof, where with time and summer sun it split and cracked like chapped lips.

Diane Funston
Break Time

I sit in the picnic park,
lunchtime from the working day.
Sport-utility vehicles flank my Corolla,
absorbing the sun with their noon-time mass.

Blond children burst from Explorer's doors,
trekking across plastic playground
towards a serpentine tunnel slide.
I eat my sandwich, chomp on cold cuts,
smile and nod to younger mothers
at a different table.

"Bill—Bob—Ben—got his promotion last month,"
say the moms, sipping Snapple, watching the kids climb higher.
"The vacation to Colorado—Connecticut—Cape Cod—was superb.
Oh, Ashley—Alicia—Allison—don't tear your Oshkosh
On rusty public swings.
Sorry girls, it's just the stress
from the remodeling,
the workers are taking longer
than I *imagine a job* could take."

They remain animated in parallel conversations.
I get up, crumble wax paper,
pack my recyclable drink bottle
in my Arctic Cooler bag.
I pull my car from between trendier shadows,
drive back to the working world.

Later, I enter my apartment door.
Later still, after clients—children—clothes washing—
I sit at my desk

seething silent stanzas,
aimed at blanket paper,
like lawn darts landing
in suburban backyards.

Louie Clay
Public Laundromat

Melissa Grossman
Driving Home

She haunts me, this young woman I drove home one evening.
Wan with hollow cheeks and mussed blond hair that fell over her face,
she kept me captive in my car, told stories about the room
she rented in a big house where no one talked to her.
She stared at a box of Girl Scout cookies on the floor by her feet,
so I gave her one. Watched her from the corner of my eye,
hold it to her mouth with both hands, like a mouse.
We arrived at the house where she lived, and I waited for her
to open the car door, but she kept talking and talking and talking—
wanting something from me I was afraid to give.
A half-hour later, she finally opened the door, then
turned back to look at me, and said thank you.
As she stepped out, I grasped the steering wheel, relieved
to drive away. A startling knock on the window made me stop.
She was still there, bending down to say thank you again,
but I knew she was really saying, please.

Kay Sundstrom
Abandoned Warehouse

I cut myself on the jagged edge of a green bean can,
swooping my fingers around the curved tin,
trying to find whatever was left,
a swift rounding of the sky. You tried to swab the bleeding,
old newspapers, junk mail, a used tampon.
But I have learned not to bleed much.
People will pay attention.

This morning we found a pizza a stiff half moon of red coral.
Maybe the kid died before he ate the rest.
Still the cut throbs and sings to me, a prophecy.
This is all we will ever be.

Afternoons we sit in the corner, surrounded by peeling tires,
torn mites of rubber, the thoracic legs of Goliath beetles.
They eat sap with briery tarsi.
I wish I had nectar sticky claws instead of fingertips,
ragged dirty crescent moon nails. By the pricking of my thumbs...
But we already know evil.

You let me tell you stories of a baby rhino named Ellen.
She is wonderful and built a raft with her best friend, a giraffe.
You inch closer to me until we nest,
a bundle of discarded T-shirts, jeans, pulled thread sweaters
we found scattered around a "Save the World" charity box.
Even the box didn't want them. No salvation for them.

Gently you pull my head to rest against your shoulder.
"It will get better," you whisper. I say nothing, kiss your hands,
listen to pulsing lullaby of my cut. It will be this.
If I open my eyes all I could see would be a shaft of light
slowly narrowing until it is nothing.

LeAnne Hunt
Tap Your Foot to Jazz; Bluegrass Will Kill You

The twang will rust your throat shut. It is Kentucky
after all. Sorrow rises with the water table. Drink your
blues away, smoke your nihilism into a fog,
but avoid bluegrass. It seeps into the skin
through the pores. Hardship and hard times and
betrayal and breakdown—these clog the lungs and
coat the tongue like coal dust.
Bluegrass digs deep. It is country
with a slap, home with a crying toddler and
jealous husband, a palm red and callused with work
and a ring finger with only a groove
left to show. Bluegrass is folks brought
down low. It is dogs fighting over
the pickings of a life. Choose the slow burn
of whiskey. Bluegrass is not safe.

John Brantingham
The Little Dancer, Aged 14, Edgar Degas

"Commentators like Vizentini and Mahalin referred openly both to the appearance and private behavior of individual ballerinas, their published remarks about 'elegant knees,' 'large lips,' and a dancer's 'embonpoint' offering a virtual directory of available charms." –Richard Kendall

Socialites loathed Degas for his dancer.
Those who thought the statue was of a real girl
hated her in her exercise clothes,
unwashed, looking tired. They wanted her
elegant, charming, willing, ready for
them. Fourteen was the age when they were no
longer called rats, when they were forced to go
on the stage for precoital dances before
the men who would buy them. I hope he
truly was their protector, the only man
in that world who'd stand for them, who kept
his hands off these children. Even today around me—
this afternoon in the gallery—she still stands
patiently as people bend to look up her skirt.

JL Martindale
Polluted

I am from gravel roads dreaming of black silk asphalt
adorned by unruly roses and lemon trees
with thorns that pierce ears
like soft plastic balls from supermarket cages.

I am birthday banana seat bicycles,
quad roller skates, garage bands and disco
backyard barbecues, barefoot climbing
stubbed toes and tangerine tree bee stings.

I am peace, love, and plastic baggies
passed over neighbors' fences,
a home-grown smoke-ring commune
of garbage heap philosophers
feeling, finally, unburdened of being.

I am fault lines, ruptured overpasses,
plaster patches hiding holes over headboards
white powder picture glass catastrophe,
film canisters lost   between   couch cushions.

I am death threats over eight balls
and dish-water blonde crystals
fractured collar bones, shrieking infants,
I am choking on my sister's birth defects.

I am valium heat-stroke epiphanies
that land us in sticky orange chairs
stuck waiting on social services to play God.

I am fresh starts, drowning
under new boyfriends she tells us to call dad
handled by hairy gurus with leering dicks like fists
that rise when they're happy.

Rise when they're angry
rise when they're drunk
rise watching me, that five year old child
dancing beneath sprinklers,
wearing fading Wonder Woman Underoos.

Annie Freewriter
No Place to Sleep

Peggy Dobreer
Little House On The Prairie Christmas

In a Little House On The Prairie special,
the bundled family shows up unexpected
in a one-horse wagon. They pray before they
eat the hand neck broke turkey Pa carried
home slung over his shoulder on snowshoes.
Pa ties a rope from the house to the barn
'cause you can't see not an arm's length and
nobody's going nowhere in that mess and
there's always enough blankets around, and
always wood in the pile and that's how it is
in the TV version.

And in my LA county Christmas there are
twelve sets of outdoor colored lights
all winking and blinking in the courtyard.
And all the streetwise little homies in the alley
are listing their Christmas jack and electronic loot
and balking at whose mom they'll get to drive
them here or there or make them snacks tonight.
Because it's just much safer to have them in
off the streets and next to your heart. And they can
wrap you right around their little fingers 'cause
they know you think like that.

This is the Christmas I know on the outskirts of
LA, on the west side of acceptable poverty.
We hunker down against the cold weeks of vacation,
put on an extra sweater and put up a pot of soup
and a ten-dollar, night-before Home Depot tree.
And we hold vigil against the nearness of life on
the street, and we hold dear the ones we know
who are already there. And we hold in contempt

the ones who have made it to New York Wall Street
wealth and turn up their noses, and think they've
seen LA if they've been to Universal City Walk
and stepped over the stars on Hollywood Boulevard.

And then we're eating turkey tetrazzini for as many
days as we can stretch it and making modified
January payments because you want those few
special moments when they're kids, and holidays
come but once a year. But you're not a kid anymore,
and when you look up, you see a sky obstructed
by a gigantic fizzling transformer
ushering us into an early grave.

And then we have to stop looking at anything
stop before we lose heart and perspective.
So we pick up a pen and write it all down because
it is more glamorous to call yourself a poet than
to call it like you see it and pretend it won't always
be this way. And I don't need yet another part-time job
or a clean-shaven man, not even another dream standing
up on its hind legs and begging to be actualized. All
I need is a metaphor and someone who can listen, and
doesn't mind if I want to be myself and tell it true.
Just like it is here on the outskirts of LA
wrapped in an extra sweater in front of a no cable TV set
at noon and calling it vacation for no other reason
than there won't be another contract 'til after the first
of the year, when this particular Little House episode
is over and done.

Clifton Snider
L.A. Is Burning

In Long Beach I sit on the periphery
of anarchy exploding in South Central Los Angeles,
spreading like contaminated air
to Hollywood, Pasadena, Compton,
perhaps to my own living room. Sirens
& helicopters break a quiet too still
to be a natural thing. The scent of fire
smudges the atmosphere.
                              Tonight
I remember twenty-seven years ago.
Watts ignited terror in the suburbs then,
burned itself into ignominy, peopled
the neighborhood with pockmarks of pain.

Tonight twelve non-black jurors in Simi Valley
confine L.A. County to house arrest while
the smoldering fire of a long recession
flares in the hands of children from every age, every
race, all poor & angry, grabbing anything worth dying for:
a garden hose, a portable TV, sundry auto parts, a VCR.

The cops beat a King into bloody black submission,
his face made to resemble a black Quasimodo,
their phallic batons held aloft
like the Pledge of Allegiance.

Our National Anthem whirls in the sky tonight.
Looters, cops, TV stations vie for attention.
The smoke rises to greet them,
and someone shoots a firefighter.

Chris Fradkin
A Merciful God

Gun Range Targets Made To Resemble Trayvon Martin
'Sold Out In Two Days'

—*The Huffington Post, May 11, 2012*

A headline so refreshing. It suggests that—if there is a god—that he or she is a merciful god, and (thank goodness and thank god) not a sane god. A sane god—after all—would've torched the planet clean upon glancing at the headline, and would've written mankind off as a mistake.

Leigh White
Kelly Thomas

Malke Singer
hella fewer helicopters

since Occupy tents
are gone
th'neighborhood
is silenter
but foreclosures
continue on in Oakland

now Richmond, California
is buying mortgages
helping citizens
stay home.

in Oakland and Baton Rouge
cities all over the globe
are shopping cart
and doorway alcove poor
families living in cars
tents of the young camped
under freeway overpasses

so many ragged
hearts where home is

Mark A. Fisher
Dog in a Shopping Cart

On the street, the old man slowly pushed a shopping cart filled with all he owned. Including his dog, a small brown mutt, riding along with lolling tongue. They traveled by, watched by so many staring eyes along that sidewalk gauntlet. A woman whined, heard by all, "That poor pup, he has no toys, no good food to eat." Passersby, dog lovers all, nodded their heads in seeming sympathy with that thought. Yet as the old wrinkled hand reached out and gave his head a pat, the dog knew. He just knew that man was his, and what they had, what little they had, they shared. What more could any dog want?

they had time
all the time in the world
together

Steve Ramirez
Open Letter to Crazy Horse, posted in the Los Angeles Times, May 1st, 1978

Dear Mr. Horse,

Please leave my husband alone. He tells me you show up at the trailer park his parents call a reservation. Says you gather around the tires they burn when the snow begins to fall like ash and you talk to them about the future.

I don't need to find my husband in the bathtub, weeping like a broken cloud. He has a job. He can tell you how many miles you have on your car by the sound of the ignition. My husband has a son, who doesn't need his father driving around town, saying graffiti is a modern version of a smoke signal.

Don't fill his head with the past. It's already a landfill where we bury our hopes. You didn't bring any magic beans with you, just a couple six packs and a lot of words. You aren't the first man to bring us old words painted like new cars with no engine under the hood.

You think you can rise from the dead like Jesus and haunt us like Catholicism. You act like there's a magic button we can press to raise the movie screen on the last two hundred years, so we can cut the cake and yell "Surprise!" But it doesn't mean we need you. It doesn't mean we want you.

We were doing fine when you were dead. Please, stay that way.

Love,
Mary

Phillip Larrea
Going Down to Wall Street

Pigs and sheep jostle
shoulder to shoulder.

Electrical prod
In cramped subway cars.

Feted for what waits.

Inexorable, this
block by block decline.

Eighteenth Street. Fourteenth,
Eighth, Fourth, gate by gate
till they hit the Wall.

Brian Coe
One Man's Trash

Katie Dwyer
Heat

In Honduras, heat and sadness were the dominant aspects of my days. The sadness I invited—I had come to seek out stories of family separation and hardship, and lived daily with the reasons people would leave their country in pursuit of mine. But the heat was a surprise in its aggression as it seeped into every motion, every interaction, until I could not disassociate the sensation of damp, desperate sweat from the slow process of recording narratives.

In the buses we pressed up against one another, one solid, sweating mass of humanity in a creaking American school bus. The young men hung from the open door in the baking dust or hot tropical rain, on the edge and in the elements. Again and again a seatmate, or someone standing face to the shoulder of my foreign height, would ask what I was doing in their country. I would answer with a shortened version of the complicated truth—I was a student doing research, and a volunteer with a Honduran organization supporting migrants and deportees.

Then, skin against skin, sharing sweat, my fellow passenger would ask if I knew how she could find her brother/cousin/sister/ son, who had been heard from last at the border of Tejas, some time ago. And, in a heat more intimate than that between lovers, I would take down a phone number and anticipate my search through prison databases and immigration detention rosters, searching for the carefully-spelled-out name scribbled on a crumpled piece of paper. Then I would make the phone call in the scant relief of the evening: "I'm sorry, I didn't find anything. God be with you." Or, both better and worse, "your son/nephew/sister/ neighbor is alive and you can contact them. But they are incarcerated and you have to follow these directions to call..."

I was an anomaly; a sweating foreign entity speaking oddly inflected Spanish. I'm sure I was the topic of many conversations, and that my reputation for 'finding' the disappeared preceded me. I had come seeking migration stories and they swarmed me—I never encountered a person without family living somewhere in my country of origin, or somehow lost along the way. Even successful migration stories were shot through with loss, as success meant that the money arrived but the relative was far away and often living precariously at the fringe of my society.

"He washes dishes but sometimes they do not pay him," I was told, and "sometimes he is thrown out of his house even though he paid in advance." "They are too scared to say anything to an authority." And I could understand why: all around me was evidence of the precarious prosperity of a loved one's successful departure, as well as the grim and silent desperation of those whose migrants had failed.

The stories overwhelmed me. The sadness was as constant as the heat.

Any relief was incomplete, lifted sometimes by watching American movies dubbed in Spanish with my host family, and being teased that the sun and mosquitoes both favored me. We sat on a concrete slab out of doors and images of my homeland played on an expensive TV, bought on credit, as the half-starved chickens scratched at the dinner scraps and the neighborhood kids laughed or were silent. Children's shows from the Disney Channel played on repeat, the simplicity and polished colors on the screen dissonant with my surroundings: verdant desert lines of palm oil plantations in what used to be farmland.

The only break from the heat came for a brief breath of time in the night. I'm sure my body was reacting to a change in temperature in the moderate cool of evening, but each night I would go to sleep sweating, only to jerk awake sometime in the night shaking with cold. There were no blankets—why would there be?—so I would curl under a bath towel and shake until I could sleep again. I never mentioned this discomfort to my hosts—they were witness to the public nature of my struggle through the heat, so I suffered the cold in private.

I don't know whether my sadness could be described as known or hidden, but such emotion was common and appropriate there. Like the heat, it surrounded me. It was all around me, and was not mine anyway—it found me because I invited it: traveled the long distance and accepted the heat and weight of stories. For those whose narratives I recorded, loss and sadness were simply fact, noted but not remarkable until a sheltered, sweating foreigner was there to be surprised.

It is difficult, now, to say how each has remained with me. Heat is forgotten—the sunburn flakes away and what is left is skin that is damaged but appears beautiful, deliberately bronzed, refreshed.

Perhaps it is the same with sadness. The storytellers are now distant but the memories remain, burning just under my skin.

Isaac Chavarría
mi cuidad

is dead like 21 children
in a historic bus accident.
como los niños swimming in canals,
falling into canals,
or dumped in them.

dead like the man shot
by a police officer in self-defense.
like immigrant refugees dehydrating
for a better life
not better victims.

dead like a coyote
shot at the Aziz-
by a rival attempting to steal
his load.

dead like my parent's
marriage, a few of my relationships,
ese huizache tree
i chopped and burned
but always returning
for me
love lies,
mis celos,
y este corazón.

Adios, Alton.
rest in peace
y ay nos vemos.

Marc Humpert
Ocean View

Robert L. Woo

Soles of my shoes scream,
Flap, Flap, Flappity, Flap, Flap,
Father's glue wore out.

Vincent Joseph Noto
The Interlopers: Carver Middle School, Fresno, California

It's 1987. I'm a substitute teacher assigned to in a middle school conjoined, like a Siamese twin, with an elementary school on the corner of Martin Luther King Jr. Boulevard and Church across the street from *the projects*. I've only been here once before. In the teacher's lounge at lunch a heated debate about equality of opportunity raged, the bell rings making it fifth period and we go separate ways. In the classroom now, after roll, we're testing. I hear a commotion outside. Students far down the hall—not really dressed for P.E. because there is no gym and no shower at this backward, under-funded school—have discovered something. It takes me a moment to make it out. Clinging high on the pale, stuccoed wall, a black bat cowers. *Where is their coach?* I wonder. The bat, upside-down to us, claws at the side of a classroom. The children throw things at it. I go back in search of a telephone. The vice principal, Mr. Love, will handle this. Then I remember—the phones are out at this broken school. I stick my neck out the door and look again. The little mob, frantic now, no longer laughing, fills with fury. Fierce, clipped shouts of "Get'm!" and "Kill it!" sharply suspend in the air, and a feral look enters the boys' eyes. They throw stones and, I think, a pair of street-shoes with laces roped together and swung like bolas, at the dark intruder which tries, blinded, screeching, in the bright light of day, to flap away or to some higher ground. I shout something, anything, about moving along back to where they are supposed to be. Only one or two of the youngest take me seriously and move off, the rest know they can ignore a sub, an interloper, like an unconscious thought. Attention fixed only on the bat. They strike out at it, dark and lean, and hit, again and again. I can't leave my class. I can't let my class know what's going on. It's over in an instant. The bat falls dead or dying. The coach calls out. The boys move along. My kids finishing their tests, ask about the noise. As if of its own volition the door flaps loose from its anchoring bolt, low on the wall, and I let it slam.

Susan Lefler
The Rodeway Inn

A skim of snow lingers in the parking lot of the Rodeway Inn, just sold. The county's crisis van stands by to offer help to those who call this home. Nell's in charge. She calls the neighbors here her congregation. Pro bono lawyers walk from door to door and knock, hoping to convince the residents that the law, for once, is not a threat to them; hoping to make clear what rights they have as tenants.

Nell moved in with her husband fifteen years ago. They shared one room stuffed with easy chairs, tables, and a little stove. It was their home until he died. Now, she's formed a protest group. She tells her people: *They'll have to let us stay.* Joan and her pit bull nod in agreement. Marge chimes in about her large mixed dog, two cats, and asthma. Joe lives with his grandmother in Room 201. She says he's a little crazy but so sweet. Jan makes mac and cheese on a hot plate for her kids. *We're only playing house,* she tells them. The weekly paper uses *they* and *them,* remote pronouns, the very ones we choose when speaking of people lost, the bruised, those we forgot, while keeping antecedents far removed.

This was once the Imperial Motel, white columns, brass doorknobs, hand painted sign. And then it fell on hard times, changed its name, began to rent the rooms from month to month to people who were out of options. Now the town must figure what to do with them, except for one young man who borrowed a tent and walked into the nearby national forest, hoping to find a kind of guarantee (sans benefits) of freedom.

Angelica Nuñez
Curtis the Nomad

Terry Ann Wright
For the Not Yet Missing

Don't be a 14-year-old girl
in the company of an adult male,
even if it's recorded that you "left of your own accord."

Don't be an 18-year-old boy. And
don't be a 24-year-old man.
Definitely don't be asked to leave a bar, even if the bouncer
remembers you and your jacket and your shoes.

Don't take your car and if you do,
don't leave it by the side of the road
with all of the windows rolled down.

Don't go fishing.
Don't go camping.
Don't go hiking.

Don't be an ex-girlfriend.
Don't be picked up outside of your home.
Don't be dropped off a block from your destination.

Whatever you do, don't be elderly,
and certainly don't have dementia or Alzheimer's.
If you do, don't take walks or live near a swamp.

Don't be a two-year-old. Don't have
a non-custodial parent from another country.
Don't have children with a citizen of any other country but yours.

Don't be bipolar. Don't be schizophrenic.
Don't be depressed. Whatever you do, don't stop
taking your meds three days before you're last seen.

Don't go to sleep. Don't take a nap.
Don't go to a convenience store.
Don't run out of gas.

Be someone who someone else saw jump off a bridge.
Be in a relationship that's "volatile." Be the expert sailor
who somehow missed the storm warning.

At least then loved ones might have a pretty good idea
where you went and maybe then
they can sleep at night.

Part Five: Soul

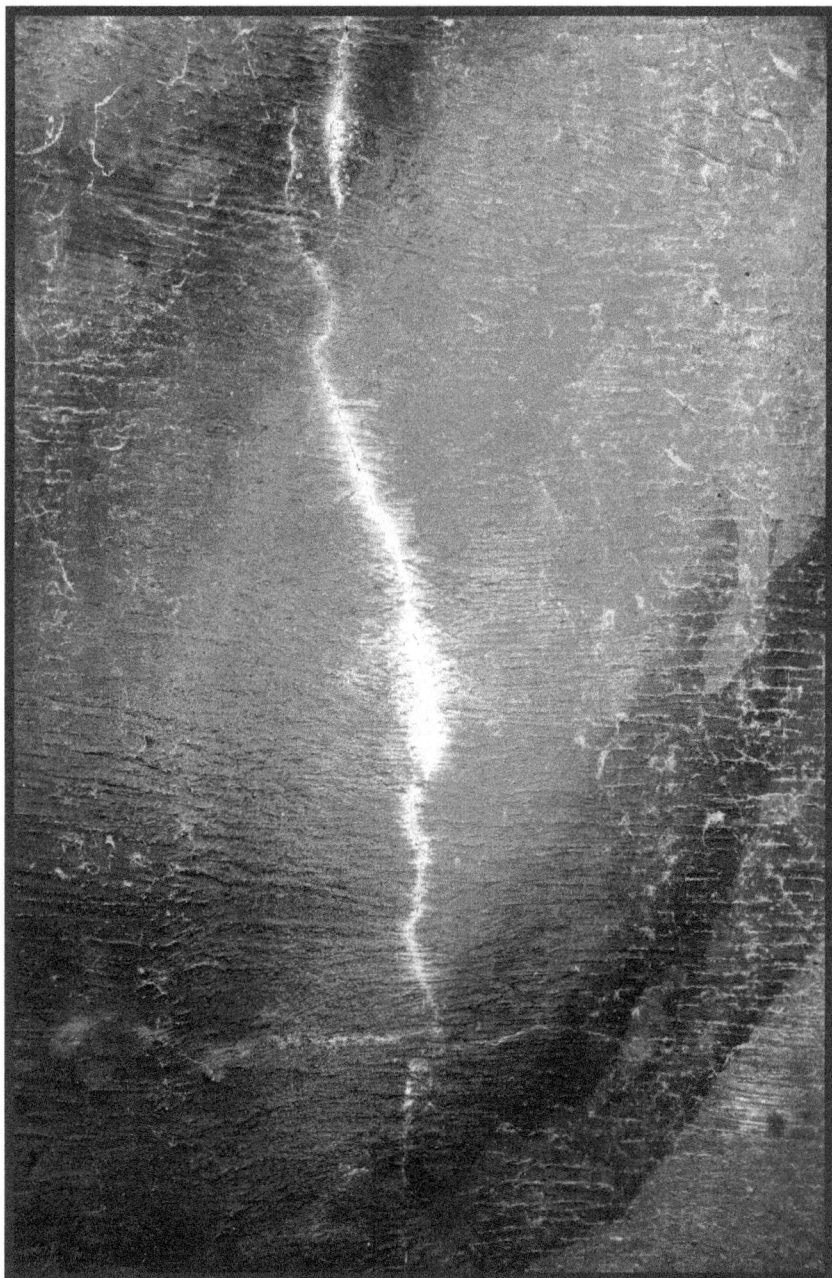

Anthony Khayat
The Mosaic

Keep,
modern lands, your white picket fences.
Keep
your Disney romances
your fat-dad-hot-mom sitcoms
with three kids—the bimbo, the smart one, and the weird one.
Keep
your network TV handcuffs
chaining the plot to some fanciful equilibrium.

Give me
your tired
your depressed
your first-time gym members
collapsing under the weight of a barbell,
the ones flying off the treadmill
ready to retire their running shoes for good.

Give me
your mid-twenties virgins
whose only dates are a computer screen
and a box of tissues.

Give me
your women who only feel safe at night
holding their keys between their knuckles
and the ones who learned that the hard way.

Give me
your recovering alcoholics
with friends who wonder why they can't
just stop at "a little buzzed."

Give me
the ones who fantasize about jamming a gun
under their chin every day but somehow manage
to keep the image imaginary.

And give me
the families and friends
of the ones who didn't manage.

Give me your PTSD veterans, your mothers and fathers who've had to pick out their children's coffins, your repentant felons bagging groceries for the rest of their lives, your obese forced to wear their vice on their body.

Give me your artists and entrepreneurs, desperately grasping onto the tattered remains of their latest idea.

Give me the ones with the single-digit bank balances, who don't know the smell of a steak dinner, and the ones who picked money over happiness because they just didn't know any better at the time.

Give me your autistic, your socially anxious, your Clippers fans, vegetables, workaholics, chocoholics, anorexics, philosophy majors, mentally scarred, physically scarred, your homeless, your hapless, your friendless, your clueless.

Hand them all over.

I want to dig you out of the cracks and crevices
of the two-story villa with the white picket fence.

Every single one of you.

And I want to stick you in
a mosaic together
—the largest the world's ever seen—
        and wake up the dreamers
            so they can marvel
                at the pebbled pattern
                    that makes up
                        our rocky reality.

Fernando Gallegos
I never felt different

I thought blocks of cheese delivered
from a nondescript white truck was normal
Crowds gathered behind, while the doors were drawn up,
waiting for cheese
I thought standing in a long line for free summer lunches
at Silverado park was the norm
Everybody was there so it was cool

Who didn't pay for full fat milk, cereal, white bread and eggs
with patriotic tickets
Statue of Liberty gloriously holding up a torch

I thought shopping at the Purple Heart thrift shop
on Santa Fe Ave was de rigueur
Bell bottom plaid pants tucked above my belly
and yellow-and-white striped long-sleeved polos
were what was "in"
Right?

I never felt different

Except maybe
when I wore a sweatshirt with Bob's name on the front
B O B didn't spell F E R N A N D O

I never felt different

But there was the one time
when I saw my friend Mario walking down Baltic Ave
towards Stephens Middle School
I waited near the door until he passed
our motor home parked outside my grandparents' house
power cord hanging overhead

Maybe I felt a little different

But mom's love, cereal and Saturday morning cartoons
kept me happy

Karineh Mahdessian
they say

home is where the heart is.
1
i'd like to know who they are
And
2
what if there is no heart.

what of us who
roam streets.
playing dominos with moon
and whisper secrets to stars

perhaps
late at night
as our heads rest upon roots
drunken teen kick us awake
or
officers hand-cuff our dreams
or
we learn to make do with what we got
and
simply
turn to stone.

Graham Smith

a lifetime's treasures
piled in plastic bags on a
borrowed shopping cart

Yvonne M. Estrada
Walking on Water

Gregory Stapp
String Theory for Crack Addicts

Everything you move is a sound;
you slough off your clothes.
See your shoes slung over a wire;
walk toward children who turn
   their backs to you.

All of your hymns are psalms of slums,
   your steps patter like plastic,
   spasms become halls of noise.

Everything's swollen; fingers wrapped
around your deliquescent arm come apart
at your touch, drip to the floor.
Turn away, the dark matter moves
   the stars and everything.

All of the universe sings a garbled lullaby,
   stars open their volcanic throats,
   moons peddle their cheap light.

Everything you wave your hands over
like a lost child hangs in front of you
like paper clouds orbiting on strings.
What you wait for revolves around you
   but never moves any closer.

All of the strings on your fingers remind you,
the echoes of people you knew tell you,
you can't remember everything,
   dark matter moves you.

Austin Eichelberger
On Colonialism

Haseya has a horse within her, a flash as bright as lightning
a dappled mare, belly jeweled with the crooked symbols
grandmother used to scratch in dirt from the steps of her double-wide
on the reservation that echoed with gunshots and addicts' moans
the place where, despite bit between teeth and leather against ears,
Haseya learned to run, to buck and jump and snort
and disappear across the plains like a retreating promise of rain.

Forrest Valdiviez
Free

The hippie in
the cowboy hat
smiled and asked for a smoke.

He said you
could meet
crazy people
at bus stations.

Just the other day
a hobo
told him
train hoppers
were 2,000 strong.

They leapt
at boxcars
to be free,
because
they were
free.

They felt like
gods
wind in hair,
roar
in ears
life in their
own hands.

Most were coordinated
but some were not.
They missed their jumps
slipped

on the tracks
           lost limbs.

Those men were
not gods,
he said.

But
at least
they
were
free.

<u>Louie Clay</u>
New Orleans 9th Ward

Ricki Mandeville
Not Quite Gone

I imagine that I do not hurt anymore,
that I am not hungry.
That climbing roses have covered me,
prettied me with pale pink
buds and blossoms, fallen petals.
I drift, as though I had opened a jar,
lured time inside, closed the lid.
It's snug here, almost cozy. I love
my solitude, now that the streets
have faded away. The absence of noise,
except for the sough of wind above me,
the shush and sway of branches.
I'm not lonely now, and I don't ache
don't think, don't remember. Soon
I'll be a dried-up heart, a tangle of hair,
a naked femur of shocking white.
The bones of an open hand grasping
toward what was out of reach.

Steve Ramirez
My Father Sings a Lullaby to His Children One Night While in Jail

The moon is a rumor, slivers
of light smuggled from the

other side of the wall, slipping
past the guards, the towers,

the dogs, the same way
I whisper thin memories

to my cell mate, hiding you
in the cavern of my skull.

Once, the bottle was a river,
carrying me away.

If I had one now, I swear
I'd drink my way back to you.

Robert Jay
Recycling Karma

Old Sue approaches my studio apartment
Leaning into her cart of aluminum cans
Like a sherpa layered in the clothing
And crucial supplies for urban survival

Her face shines forth a tireless grin
Cheekbones rising up like Himalayan foothills
Lidded eyes look about to survey the scene
Of our local streets and alleyways

Smiling through her palms
Pressed together in gratitude
She could be a patron saint
Or laughing bodhisattva

Looking about my pad
I search for anything of worth
To give her without a second thought
Of karma or conditional rewards

Fruits and vegetables soon spoiled
Beer cans and spare change
So much excess taken for granted
In my middle-class lifestyle

Offering up empty cans of PBR
and Tecate from my littered patio
Once fuel to get me through
This lifetime's Realm of Hungry Ghosts

Now serve as empty remnants
Crushed into the currency of the streets
To be recycled into their next life
As the same Samsara cycle continues

As Old Sue collects the value
Of each can with a smile, hands
Together in sincere gratitude
We have a good arrangement

She bestows blessings upon me and I drink
To keep up with the current state of poverty
Waiting for these empty cans to culminate
In the relief of our suffering

Robert Jay
Old Sue

Sarah Thursday
Why I Can't Kill Daddy Longlegs Hiding
in My Shower Curtain

Because I know he is home-seeking and hungry.
Because I see the fragility of eight legs holding tight to porcelain.
Because I once needed to be scooped up from drowning
        showers to sunlit window panes.
Because when I was nine, I had to break into our motel room on
        a Friday night after church.
Because my mom forgot to pick me up, but I knew she was just
        sleeping inside.
Because I didn't have a key and I was sure she'd be right back.
Because the windows were slats of louvered glass, I could pull
        them apart and lay them gently on the asphalt driveway.
Because I was small, could slide between three removed slats, and
        land on a mattressed floor.
Because I'd rather sleep alone in a tiny motel room with navy-blue
        carpeted halls leading to the tenants' communal bathroom.
Because calling my father
        was not an alternative.
Because I knew my mother would come home soon even after I fell
        asleep under a curtain of blankets.
Because I knew if I was quiet I could be safe enough.
Because I couldn't have driven myself home from church or climbed
        up the window alone.
Because someone had to scoop me up to push me through it.

Annie Freewriter
The "Situation"

I was in a hurry the other day while on the way to the nursing home to check on my dad. At Target, I read through my mental list: "Glass water jar for fridge, feminine pads (buy three and save $5, the sign read), and last, a denture brush for my dad." Oh darn, no brush, so on to try Rite Aide next. I lost my footing in Rite Aide when I saw the spinning tower of sunglasses, then I found the brush, and then I thought, "Okay, now focus on the exit...wait...gum on sale, 3 for $1 each. Okay, done. Next, Trader Joe's."

My mental list continued with, "Carrot juice and water. Do not stop to browse." But then, I heard this sweet little voice in front of me, coming from the seat of a shopping cart, "Mommy, can we get some apple crushers, please?" The mom, pushing her two little boys, about 4 and 6 years old, said, "I'm sorry honey, we're in a 'situation' right now and we need to be careful." The boy's round little face drooped but he didn't whine. I pulled out my wallet and counted five of the ten dollar bills I had. I folded them and, as I passed the little boy in the cart, pressed the money into his limp hand. "Here, this is for you," I said. I then proceeded to the checkout with my carrot juice and water.

Oh yes, I could have judged this mother with her two clean, well-dressed, rosy-cheeked boys. In fact, my first thought was, "So what are you doing shopping at Trader Joe's?" But you see, I've been in many "situations" with my own three precious little dependents. And yes, I was judged. I was even condemned to hell by some. I was shunned by my "family" of church-goers and by my family of origin. The lawyers who snickered behind closed doors, the judge with his gavel of indifference, the lack of eye contact by the passersby near the food line while waiting for my block of cheese and fluffy white bread. But little did they know what I was made of. Grit, tenacity, perseverance and mother-bear love—that's what I was made of.

Someone shared a video on Facebook recently about a mother bear that had brought her three little cubs to scavenge in a green dumpster. The cubs were able to get in but unable to get out. Some kind people in a truck lowered a ladder into the bin and then pulled away to give the cubs space to climb out and join their frantic mother pacing nearby. It was heartwarming to see them shuffle off with their happy mother into the safety of their home—the woods.

The first "situation" pushed me out of the comfort of our home in 1981, after a sale sign was plunked like a dagger into the front yard. This was after I signed the papers for the divorce "situation." We had to leave "the woods," in search of food and shelter. For years I bounced from job to job, and from house to house, while I clutched my children like helium balloons. I was just trying to keep them anchored until our "situation" changed. I held onto hope like a climber holding onto the ledges of a cliff, with fingertips and toes.

I found a job at a vitamin factory and took a bus to work—eleven miles each way—until I saved enough for a used bicycle. The only rental I could afford for months was our "dumpster"—a motel for the "low-lifes," or as they would say today, "losers." It was a two-story rectangular building with rooms the size of jail cells, with just enough space for two mattresses, L-shaped and squeezed against the wardrobe and sink. One small window let in a pallet of hazy light by day, and a single bulb bounced light off our heads at night. We spent afternoons at the library, our sanctuary, doing homework and reading.

One day, the heat was so intense on my walk home from work (because sometimes I didn't have bus fare) that I began to hear ringing in my ears and pedestrians' voices became too muffled to distinguish. I stumbled into a restaurant. I slumped onto the bench in a booth and laid my face against the cool table. A kind-faced waitress approached me with a glass of cool water. "Here," she said, "drink this." She patted my hand and whispered, "Stay here as long as you need to."

Then, after I bought my used Schwinn bicycle, I stored it in the only available floor space, which meant that we had to step across it to reach our beds. My daughters shared a mattress and I slept on the other. The tenant-shared bathroom in the motel was so filthy we had to carry a rag and a can of Lysol every time we used the toilet, and a can of cleanser for the bottom of the shower. This "dumpster" was located in the city of Lomita in a "third-world" part of town. We ate whatever we could from a box or bag (I didn't own a can-opener). Fortunately, my children were able to eat school lunches. One time, I was so desperate for a hot meal that I pulled in my claws and rode to my ex-husband's house on my bike to ask if he could heat our can of soup. The answer was a door in my face. My claws came back out.

After purchasing my used Schwinn bike, life eased up a little, until they began to increase our work hours. We had to keep up with the supply and demand so the rich ladies with their full purses and coiffed hair could stay healthy. The workers couldn't afford the vitamins they bottled, so they slipped fallen ones into their aprons to take home to their families.

But the exhaustive hours finally took their toll on my body and one day I almost fell off my bike after I wobbled up to the sidewalk of a KFC. I was ushered in by a patron who yelled, "Quick, get this lady some water."

"We'll bring you some water. Please wait outside."

Everyone was staring at me. I somehow made it out the door just as my stomach began to rebel. I had a plastic bag clamped on the bike carrier. I pulled it out just as my stomach's fury arrived full force. An employee came out with a plastic cup.

"The boss said you must leave," she said firmly. "We can't allow you in front of our store."

I made my way next door to a gas station restroom, where I promptly collapsed onto the cold cement.

"Lady, you've been in there an hour. Are you okay?" The gas station attendant sounded gravely concerned. "Would you like me to call an ambulance?"

"No, no, I'll be okay," I said weakly. I slowly pushed my bike home and then curled up on my bed.

Soon after, my brother-in-law told me about an affordable place that was available to rent as soon as he moved out. It was a tiny duplex facing an alley, with one bedroom for my daughters, and a laundry room wide enough to fit a bed and dresser for my son. Our kitchen had a sink and counters, a refrigerator, a stove, and cupboards painted dark green with red centers. We had our own bathroom with a claw-footed tub, a toilet and a sink. I slept on a fold-out foam love seat, except for the times our floors were lined with children (friends and my niece). Then I slept in the closet or in the bathtub. This house became our "castle in the woods" until I was married again two and a half years later. Our situation was no longer a green dumpster, and I had finally found a way out for my cubs.

My three grown children are safe now...and I can rest. In fact, I think I'll hibernate.

Deirdre Favreau
Doll on Mattress

Ricki Mandeville
Relative Luxuries

She gets a job, finally.
A hotel near the Quarter,
ramshackle and not the best
but perfect for the budget conscious.
It is summer, the city hot,
the sky too close and radiating heat.
She rents a small room now,
sleeps face up by the window,
lets sun through the cracked pane wake her.

A room. Such luxury for the three of them
who'd lived in cardboard walls and watched
the bedroom melt in every rain,
and used a fitful hotplate
to cook the thin soup, the greens
swimming in leftover pats of butter,
smuggled home from half empty plates
to put some fat on her two skinny boys.

She walks to work in a black skirt
and a clean blouse hand washed in the rusty sink,
walks toward drudgery like it was salvation,
spends the day humming,
cleaning night from the rooms
of tight-fisted L.A. tourists,
shoes and underwear all over the floor,
handfuls of change left scattered on the dressers.
She isn't tempted any more.
She has enough for now.

Mary Buchinger
Earrings I Never Wear

In a small Bolivian town
on a narrow cobblestone path,
a woman in a black bowler hat
sits at a tiny tin table in front
of her sky-blue house selling
shiny things that would catch
a magpie's eye. I finger the glitter,

but it's the earrings she's wearing
I want—articulated fish, worn
brass, warped, greenish, hinged
with rings, a head, tail, and fins.
Do you have any like those
for sale, I ask. She shakes
her head as she pulls them
from her lobes. *My husband
made these, they take the extra
air out of your head, make it
possible to breathe, best earrings
for a headache.* She says this
as she thrusts them into my palm
and my head begins to throb.

No, I say, they're yours,
your husband made them,
they heal you, keep them,
please, I only wondered
if there were any others—
These, please. Buy these.
Already in my hand,
they curl and die.

Fernando Gallegos
Under the same moon

Here
   cold champagne, bubbles float to the surface in slow undulating dances

There
   tap water drips from rusty pipes in the still warm night

Here
   brunch @ 11 a.m., rosemary potatoes with steak omelet, drizzled with hollandaise sauce

There
   corn flakes with a spoonful of strawberry jam to add a hint of sweetness

Here
   cute little kitty scurries across the living room, making me trip

There
   the multiple roach motels welcome the scurrying new guests

Here
   wind blows across sands off Bolsa Chica, as the fire warms the air

There
   the slow fan blows across the sale aisle, bananas aren't all that black

Here
   the full moon fills the sky with a warm night glow

There
   the full moon fills the sky with a warm night glow

Marco A. Vasquez
Climb

How do oranges divide up sunlight
in the orange tree?
        –Pablo Neruda, The Book of Questions

From the breakfast table Dad
and I can see the orange
tree in our yard—our eyes squinting
from the glowing sunlight. Mugs
in hand, Dad hands me *pan dulce*
and mentions how much our tree has grown
and reminds me of how we
used to pick oranges together.

It would have been really easy
to pluck the bunches that hung
low on young branches, but Dad
insisted on climbing all the way
to the top—thick thorns scraping
white stripes onto his sun-baked
arms. He said the oranges
on top tasted sweeter. When
he climbed back down and split open
the juicy orb, handing me
my half, I would sink my face
into it and believe him.

Throughout most of my grade school
experience, I was told
I would end up in fast-food
due to my failure to turn
in homework and my incessant
truants. Dad never had the opportunity
to attend school. He worked back-breaking
labor for most of his life.

He would remind me of this
whenever he received notes
and phone calls from teachers
and counselors, then whip me,
because he felt obligated,
until I screamed in agony.

He would then go outside and climb
the tree, picking the highest
orange, split it, and place my
half in my tear-soaked hands—a sweet
apology. He eventually
taught me to climb the tree—giving
me boosts the first couple of times,
until I learned to climb it
myself.
    Now, Dad gets to rest
his retired frame and hardly
has the strength to climb the tree
at all. I do most of the climbing—
thick thorns slice red stripes on my
pale indoor arms on my way
up. Still—with a few degrees
under my belt, a satisfying
career in education,
and plenty of food on the table—
things are good. Had I opted
for the fast-food route, I would
have probably made assistant
manager by now; however, I
doubt that my coffee would taste
this warm, my pastry this flaky,
my oranges this sweet.

Tobi Cogswell
The Bench Outside the Thrift Store

is not for sale. Still shiny
with shellac in some places,

worn tired in others.
It's where he waits for Doris,

who comes in the back door
to turn the "be back clock"

around to "open" and to smile
the beacon of a thousand

lighthouses for those lost at sea
as she lets him into the warmth

to forage for just one shirt,
the perfect shade of bluish-gray.

Today he sees his daughter.
He wants a color to mirror

her eyes perfectly. She will
be pleased at her importance

to a man who some days
can only watch the clock,

think about where he'd gone lost,
and how he can now see the sky.

Rain Sheiman
Takin' in Salento

Sarah Thursday
All The Ways I Deserve You

I was excited to meet you.
You would be more like me.
All those years being yanked
from one place to the next,
being pulled out of school early
means I wasn't coming back.
I can't remember the names
of my teachers, but I can recite
cities like family members.

Then I met you, Long Beach,
the city of everything,
of Cambodia and Mexico,
of apartments spilling bodies
in the streets, spilling ranchero melodies
and clicking tongues full of Vietnam.
My color was a minority.
My clothes from donated boxes
did not flinch you—
you with your narrow alleyways
and grubby-cheeked children.

I was at home before I knew
how long I'd stay. I knew you
were like me, born of struggle
and sitting on windowsills staring
out at distant city lights.

Even when we got a new father
and lived among your riverside homes,
it was all wrong like me.
Concrete banks dressed in graffiti.

Wilderness trails where teenage boys
played war around stained mattresses
left by public refugees.

I became a woman in your sunlight.
I never had to deserve you.

You knew all my names,
even when I left you.
I tried to be the golden boardwalks
of Hermosa and Redondo
but they pushed me out
to the gum-stained sidewalks
of Lawndale, where train tracks
drew lines between me and him,
where girls like me paid their own way
through city college.

Then he left me for Westwood,
a place I could never see
my own stark reflection,
so I came home to you,
and the best skin of you.

I wore my new clothes here
on all your borders north
and south, and east and west.
All your contradictions sang
like love songs, even when for years
I was only your mistress.

Other cities have soccer moms
and radio-friendly punk rock,
winter tans and French manicures,

but I know, even they find a place
in your diagonals, your Wardlows
that cross both apartment projects
and gated communities.

I will grow old here, far from your shore.
Even though I bought a house
next to the tracks again, your tracks
comfort me—not division but connection,
a literal line of how close we are,
side-by-side, lying in the lap of you.

Viannah E. Duncan
Widows
a found poem

One week
at a widows' conference in Bangalore
was sufficient to cause these formerly
secluded widows to put on
forbidden
colors and to apply for loans;

One elderly woman,
"widowed" at the age of seven,
danced for the
first time
in her life,
whirling wildly
in the center of the floor.

Lee Kottner
Sun After Rain in the South Bronx

The sudden sun transforms everything
even here—especially here:
scrub trees in a trash-strewn ravine
become a peridot glade behind their razor wire;
cut stone façades robe themselves in rose gold;
brick walls glow with the fire
that hardened them;
asphalt, rainwashed, glitters like snakeskin,
slithering water;
taxis quiver and run with yolky yellow;
the green of meadows veils, briefly,
the vacant lots and postage-stamp lawns
—all revealed in glory
by the simple, ready grace of light.

Terry Ann Wright
Wonder
hat tip to Phillip Larrea

I invite my best friend and her daughter, soon to leave for college,
to a park by the beach to see an outdoor screening of
An American in Paris.
It's a soft evening. There are beach chairs.
There are snacks and wine in plastic cups.
My friend lifts the hair off the back of her neck
as the sun sets, and asks,
"I wonder what poor people are doing tonight."

A few months later we are no longer friends.

I ask an acquaintance how her job search is going.
Not so well, she says. I empathize. It's hard out there.
"It's not just that," she says. "It's that I have friends
who work in hiring departments that tell me
I will never get a job because I'm White. They're all going
to Blacks and Mexicans." I look forward
to telling my students that they're taking *all the jobs*
from White people.

I think they'll be pleasantly surprised to hear it.

In a city whose motto is "the future
of Southern California," we watch people
stop a bus full of women and children in the street.
One woman says her daughter came to Tuesday's demonstration
but was spit on
and asked to clean toilets.
Is it any wonder we ask, "We are a cruel people, aren't we?"
Not them. Not you. We.

Peggy Dobreer
Selling Lime and Chili

Marco A. Vasquez
Two Intersections

1.

I give him a dollar.
He gives me the oranges.
He nods "*gracias*,"
takes off his baseball cap—
wet from the sun—wipes
his brow on his shoulder,
bringing out the original
color of the faded T-
shirt that he has owned
for years. He lifts the dollar
up against the unforgiving
rays, makes the sign
of the cross, folds the bill,
and puts it into
the pocket that feeds
his family. He goes
to the next car. If
they don't buy, he goes
to the next car. I
go when the light turns green.

2.

I stop when the light turns
red. He claims hunger
and veterancy on card-
board, in black Magic
Marker. He wears several
layers of clothing
despite the heat. He stands,

and sometimes leans, against
a pole with two empty
bottles at its base. He
pulls his pockets inside-
out to prove his need.
He extends his palm—shaking
with thirst—with the butt
of a freshly lit cigarette
sprouting from in between
his middle and forefinger.
He winks "*howdy*"
and asks me for a dollar.
I give him the oranges.

Contributor Bios & Acknowledgments

Alejandro Duarte is a devoted father of three who works with developmentally disabled adults. Alex has been a cab driver, a furniture designer, and a production manager in the fashion industry. Originally from Costa Mesa, CA, he has lived in Montevideo, Uruguay. Today, he is a member of The Poetry Lab in Long Beach, CA. His poems have appeared on *Cadence Collective*, *The Unrorean*, and he is working on *TaxiFly*, a collection of poems.

Alexis Rueal has been in the Columbus, Ohio, poetry scene since 2011. She has been published in many online and print journals, and her first chapbook, *Letter to 20*, was published by Poet's Haven Press in 2013. She was a member of the 2013 Writers' Block National Poetry Slam team and is a three-time featured poet at the Columbus Arts Festival. When she isn't writing and performing, she runs her own online wedding business and spends time with her husband and pets.

Angelica Nuñez has been a writer and artist for over 20 years. Her murals may be found in many schools in Long Beach, CA, including Alvarado Elementary and Huntington School for Boys and Girls. She was also an art teacher at one time, working with children with disabilities. She has received awards and recognition for her art. She currently resides in the Arts District in Long Beach, CA.

Annie Freewriter has her earliest memories on the prairies of Alberta, Canada. As an adult retired woman, with three adult children and two grandchildren, she discovered her ability and need to write in a memoir writing group. Her love for the memoir genre started as a teen when she read every biography and autobiography placed on her library shelf in the city of Orange. Now she's writing her own story and she won't look back until she's done. "I matter and so do you."

Anthony Khayat is a founding member of the art and creative writing website thepaperplanepilots.com, where he contributes poetry and short fiction under the moniker Ace Kingsly. He's been featured in the site's recent anthology *Reasons to Never Return*. Anthony's an L.A. man through and through—born in Hollywood, raised in Tujunga, graduated from Loyola Marymount University, works in Westwood, and lives in Redondo Beach. "The Mosaic" previously appeared in *PaperPlane Pilots*.

Austin Eichelberger is happily still teaching English and writing in New Mexico. His fiction has appeared in *Cease, Cows*, *Flash: The International Short-Short Story Magazine*, *Gone Lawn*, *Extract(s)*, *Eclectic Flash*, *First Stop*

Fiction, and others. More of his writing lives at austineichelberger.wordpress.com.

Brian Coe, in addition to shooting photography, spends his time writing, traveling, playing music & fostering relationships with nature. He believes as much in the limitlessness of imagination as the raw simplicity of cause & effect. If you build a bird feeder, birds will come.

Chris Fradkin is a former beet farmer now living in Brazil. His prose and poetry have appeared in *Monkeybicycle, Thrice Fiction,* and *Thrush Poetry Journal.* His songs have been performed by Fergie, The Plimsouls, and The Flamin' Groovies. And his Emmy-award-winning sound editorial has graced *The X-Files.* "A Merciful God" previously appeared in *Mobius: The Journal of Social Change.*

Christian Lozada's poetry and fiction can be seen in upcoming issues of *Blue Collar Review* and the *Cadence Collective: Year One Anthology* and has been in *Spot Literary Journal, Amulet, A&E Magazine,* and elsewhere. He co-authored a photographic history book, *Hawaiians In Los Angeles,* and his nonfiction works have been published in *Watermark Journal* and *Body in Paradise.* He received his MFA at California State University, Long Beach.

Christina Foskey is a Californian thrift store junkie. Her work has been published in the *San Gabriel Valley Poetry Quarterly.* The Writers' Club of Whittier Poets awarded her poem titled "The One With Untamed Hair" as winner of the annual 2014 Whittier, CA poetry contest. Her first chapbook *Eighty Degrees and Thunder* was published in April of 2014.

Clifton Snider, faculty emeritus at Cal State University, Long Beach, is the internationally celebrated author of ten books of poetry. In 2000–2001 he published three novels, *Loud Whisper, Bare Roots,* and *Wrestling with Angels: A Tale of Two Brothers.* New from Spout Hill Press is his first historical novel, *The Plymouth Papers.* A Jungian/Queer literary critic, his book, *The Stuff That Dreams Are Made On,* was published in 1991. His work has been translated into Arabic, French, Spanish, and Russian. "LA is Burning" previously appeared in *Moonman: New and Selected Poems,* published by World Parade Books.

Dan Steinbacher kept it real in some pretty sketchy parts of Long Beach some years ago. Now he enjoys going out to breakfast in slightly nicer areas, where he watches people water their sidewalks and pretend to pick up their dog poop. He writes poetry and other things when he should be working.

Daniel McGinn's work has appeared in numerous anthologies and publications, including *Bank-Heavy Press, Lummox, Silver Birch Press, OC*

Weekly, Next Magazine, Freeze Ray, Spillway, Rip Rap, Re)verb, Amethyst Arsenic and others. His full-length collection of poems, *1000 Black Umbrellas* was released by Write Bloody Press. He's had five chapbooks published as part of the Laguna Poets chapbook series. He has an MFA in writing from Vermont College of Fine Arts. He and his wife, poet Lori McGinn, are natives of Southern California. They have 3 children, 6 grandchildren, two parakeets and a very good dog. "November" previously appeared in *Re)verb*.

David S. Pointer contributes frequently to his local newspaper on homelessness, *The Contributor*. David was named a winning writer in *Empty Shoes: Poems on Hunger and Homelessness Anthology* that went to number 2 at Amazon.com in its category. David currently serves on the advisory panel of Writing For Peace.

Deirdre Favreau enjoys all the arts and especially architecture. She has been active in the four P's: Painting, Printmaking, Photography, & Poetry. Under her musician's name, Didi Favreau, she has released one LP, three CDs, and many singles..."Deal With It" being her latest CD. She currently lives in Yreka, California.

Diane Funston is originally from Rochester, New York, and now divides her time between a cabin in Tehachapi, California, and a mining town in Round Mountain, Nevada. She has been published in the *San Diego Poetry Annual, Magee Park Poets, GUTS*, and others in California and upstate New York. Her passions include gardening and dog rescue. Her literary heroes include Oscar Wilde and the Romantic poets.

Don Kingfisher Campbell earned an MFA in Creative Writing last year from Antioch University, Los Angeles. His poems have recently appeared in *..and it happened under cover, The Gambler, Oddball Magazine, Poetic Diversity, Revolutionary Poets Brigade, Sassafras, Spilt Ink, Statement*, and *Tower Journal*. He is the editor of the *San Gabriel Valley Poetry Quarterly* and host of Saturday Afternoon Poetry inside the backroom of the Santa Catalina Branch of the Pasadena Public Library.

Donna Hilbert's latest book is *The Congress of Luminous Bodies*, from Aortic Books. *The Green Season*, World Parade Books, a collection of poems, stories and essays, is now available in an expanded second edition. She is a frequent contributor to the online journal *Your Daily Poem*. Her work is widely anthologized, most recently in *The Widows' Handbook*, Kent State University Press. Learn more at www.donnahilbert.com. Both "1942 Snapshot of My Father" and "Madhill" are from her book *Mansions*.

Dr. Ernest Williamson III has published poetry and visual art in over 500 national and international online and print journals. Dr. Williamson is an

Assistant Professor of English at Allen University, self-taught pianist, editor, poet, singer, composer, social scientist, private tutor, and a self-taught painter. His poetry has been nominated three times for the *Best of the Net Anthology*.

Esmeralda Villalobos is an artist from Guadalajara, Mexico, currently living in Southern California. Her primary medias are oils and acrylics but she also enjoys working in watercolors, ink, and other mixed media. As far as her painting style is concerned, she feels experimenting with different forms—surrealism, abstract expressionism, realism—is one of the greatest freedoms an artist has. Working in different styles and media keeps her interested, engaged, and helps to expand her creativity.

Fernando Gallegos is Long Beach born and raised. The first real poem he ever wrote was a repetitive phrase that became a song that he no longer remembers. Music, poetry, and art make him who he is. Follow him at Facebook.com/Fernando.Gallegos.LBC.

Forrest Valdiviez lives in San Pedro with an angry rescue cat named Jerry Jackson Browne. They both like to chase, catch, and let things go.

G. Murray Thomas is the author of *My Kidney Just Arrived*. "Sure I've known poverty/ but only Top Ramen poverty/ not dog food poverty/ and certainly not starvation." "Coins on the Sidewalk" is published in his book *Cows on the Freeway*.

Gale Acuff's poems have appeared in many literary journals. Gale is also the author of three books of poetry. He has taught university English in the U.S., China, and Palestine, and currently teaches literature at Sichuan University for Nationalities in China.

Ginna Wilkerson completed a Ph.D. in Creative Writing at University of Aberdeen in 2013, also the year of publication of her first poetry collection, *Odd Remains*. Her photographs have been displayed in both Scotland and the US. This summer, Ginna has been in residency at Can Serrat Artist's Residence in El Bruc, Spain. Currently, she teaches at Ringling College of Art and Design.

Graham Smith is a poet and former lawyer living in Long Beach. His work has been published in *If It's Wednesday, It Must Be Haiku, A Poet Is A Poet No Matter How Tall, 50 Haikus*, and *Cadence Collective*, among others. Graham frequents local poetry readings, where he has been known to read haiku, his favorite form of poetry.

Gregory Stapp is a graduate of the University of Oklahoma, where he worked for the Carl Albert Center Congressional Archives, was a Puterbaugh

Fellow in World Literature, and won the Tomas Rivera Student Writing prize in Short Fiction. He is currently an MFA candidate at Queens University of Charlotte and his poems have appeared in *qarrtsiluni, Eunoia Review, Outside In Literary and Travel Magazine*, and *ditch*.

I.B. Rad and Mrs. Rad live in NY City with Wonderdog, who allows them the run of her house. A number of I.B.'s poems can be read (and in some cases heard) on the internet by googling "I.B. Rad and poetry." Hope you enjoy them.

Isaac Chavarría is a pocho with an MFA in Creative Writing from the University of Texas-Pan American. He enjoys assisting non-profit organizations in producing chapbooks for workshop participants. His poems are in *The Acentos Review* and *Rio Grande Review* online. His poetry book, *Poxo*, from Slough Press, received the inaugural 2014 NACCS-Tejas Poetry Award. You can find Isaac in Alton, TX.

JL Martindale is a real, live, writing mama residing in Southern California. She's a regular contributor to *Cadence Collective*, and has also published work with *Bank-Heavy Press, Micro Story a Week*, and a few now-defunct literary magazines.

Jackie Joice is an award winning photographer and author of *Green Grapes Black Hands*.

Joe Gardner was born in June of '74, in San Bernardino, CA. He was a paratrooper in the United States Army, has walked the blue collar roads of America, and has previously been published in *Modern Drunkard Magazine, San Gabriel Valley Poetry Quarterly, Cadence Collective, LUMMOX One* and *Two*. Joe is also the 2013 recipient of the Joe Hill Labor Poetry Award.

John Brantingham is an English professor and the director of the creative writing program at Mt. San Antonio College in Walnut, CA, the writer-in-residence at the dA Center for Cultural Arts in Pomona, CA, and the president of the San Gabriel Valley Literary Festival. His latest book is *The Green of Sunset* from Moon Tide Press.

K. Andrew Turner writes literary and speculative fiction, poetry, and nonfiction. He teaches and mentors creative writers. He is also the Editor-in-Chief of *East Jasmine Review* and a freelance editor. Near Los Angeles, he lives, works and writes in the San Gabriel Valley. You can find more at his website: www.kandrewturner.com

Karen Boissonneault-Gauthier is a photographer, writer and poet who has often been told she has an eye for what the camera loves. Finding the oddity within the beautiful, the spark within the mundane and capturing the nightmare as well as the dream simultaneously, is something she strives to do. Karen has shot cover art for *Crack the Spine Literary Magazine* and *Zen Dixie Magazine*, where she has a monthly column. She has been featured in *Artemis Journal, Fine Flu Literary Journal,* and *Vagabonds Anthology* to name a few of the creative places she dwells. Find her on Twitter @KBG_Tweets.

Karineh Mahdessian learned English by reading Nancy Drew books and watching *Married with Children*. She has a great affinity for really large earrings, enjoys tacos from Highland Park taco trucks, and will challenge anyone to a thumb wrestling match. Anytime. Anyplace. She is absolutely in love with haikus and is now the hostess with the mostest for La Palabra at Avenue 50 studios in Highland Park.

Karla Cordero is an MFA candidate at San Diego State University. She is a contributing writer for *Poetry International* and editor for SpitJournal.com, an online literary review for poetry. Her work has appeared in *The NewerYork, Cleaver Magazine, The California Journal of Women Writers, Bookends Review, Apeiron Review, Cease,Cows,* and elsewhere. She lives in California with her two dogs, one turtle, and a goldfish named "Fifteen Cent."

Karlee A. Tittle Cuff is a musician in the psychedelic reggaesoul melodia band Grievous Angels. Her thirst for knowledge inspired her to obtain a BA in Philosophy from CSULB. She resides in the City of Angels with her Bobby, her husband/bandmate, and their dog Nina. They dream together and enjoy the journey along the way.

Katie Dwyer is an emerging creative writer with a passion for social justice and connection. Originally from Colorado, she currently resides in Ireland where she received a master's degree in International Human Rights Law. Both her writing and advocacy work are concerned with borders and barriers, and the need for dialogue to tear them down.

Kay Sundstrom started writing after a botched spinal fusion. During the months spent in a hospital, she discovered writing, which became her passion. Since then she has worked with Thom Gunn, Adrienne Rich, and others. She was also a Stegner Fellow in Poetry. She has been published in various publications and performed a one-women show at the Climate Theatre in San Francisco. But a few years ago, she needed two brain surgeries. At first she would have to wait an hour between writing each line. But the writing flows through her again. She is so grateful.

LeAnne Hunt lives in Orange County with her daughter and a furry sphere of a cat and is a regular at the Ugly Mug reading. She was published in *LUMMOX Number Two* (LUMMOX Press, 2013) and *Cadence Collective*. She has poems forthcoming in the next issue of *Edgar Allan Poet Journal*.

Lee Kottner is a writer, educator, union activist, and book artist living in Harlem, NY. Her poetry has appeared in several journals and anthologies, and a chapbook from Blue Stone Press. *Stories from the Ruins*, a hand-bound, hardcover artist's chapbook of 16 poems about the events of 9/11, is in the permanent collections of the Detroit Institute of Arts and MoMA. She's currently working on her next poetry collection while teaching at CUNY's York College and City College of Technology and New Jersey City University.

Leigh White is an acclaimed artist and prolific poet from Southern California. She became a homeless advocate on January 13, 2014, the day of the not-guilty verdicts in the criminal trial of 2 of the 6 Fullerton Police Officers who murdered Kelly Thomas. Kelly was a gentle, homeless man who had schizophrenia and was doing nothing wrong. The civil trial begins in December 2014.

Loretta Diane Walker is a two time Pushcart nominee. She has published two collections of poetry. Her manuscript *Word Ghetto* won the 2011 Bluelight Press Book Award. Walker's work has appeared in a number of publications including *The Concho River Review, Haight-Ashbury Literary Journal, Illya's Honey, Orbis International Journal, San Pedro River Review, The Texas Observer* and *94 Creations*. She teaches music at Reagan Magnet School in Odessa, Texas. Loretta received a BME from Texas Tech University and earned an MA from The University of Texas of the Permian Basin.

Louie Clay is an emeritus professor at Rutgers. Editors have published 2,349 of his essays, poems and photographs. He lives in East Orange, NJ, with Ernest Clay, his husband for 40 years.

Maja Trochimczyk, PhD, is a Polish-born poet, music historian, and photographer. She published four books on music and four of poetry: *Rose Always, Miriam's Iris, Chopin with Cherries*, and *Meditations on Divine Names*. Her next book is *Slicing the Bread* from Finishing Line Press. A Board member of the Polish American Historical Association, she wrote hundreds of articles and poems. Find her at trochimczyk.net and moonrisepress.com. "Peeling the Potatoes" previously appeared as "Her Grandma" in *Poetry and Cookies*.

Malke Singer lives in Oakland, California. She is a 60-year-old Jewish Lesbian, an Occupational Therapist at WCCUSD, an organizer of Born to Drum Womans' Drum Camp, an adoptive mother, an advocate of peace and justice, and engaged in learning to write, drum, and grow organic food.

Marc Humpert, born and raised in Northern California by way of Swiss and American descent, is a multi-discipline artist. Since journeying to Sri Lanka for aid work, Marc continues to coordinate youth spaces with non-profits, including LA-based Imagination Foundation, and implement educational game challenges via Irvine's MIND Research Institute. Driven to maintain an awareness of the world we live in, Marc strives to problem-solve across platforms with innovation and imagination.

Marco A. Vasquez received his MFA in creative writing from California State University, Long Beach. He is the author of four collections of poetry, one of which was edited by Gary Soto as part of his Chicano Chapbook Series. His first novel, *Steven Isn't Normal*, will be published in the fall by Floricanto Press. He currently lives in Whittier, California, with his wife and two boys. "Over-time" first appeared in *Standing At The Corner Of Trouble And Sacrifice*, "Hiding The Evidence" first appeared in *East L. Alien*, "Climb" first appeared in *Disorient magazine*, and "Two Intersections" first appeared in *Pearl Magazine*.

Mark A. Fisher is a writer, poet, and playwright living in Tehachapi, CA. His column "Lost in the Stars" has appeared in Tehachapi's *The Loop* newspaper for several years. His plays have appeared on stages in Pine Mountain Club, Tehachapi, and Hayward. His poetry has appeared in A *Sharp Piece of Awesome*, *The Antelope Valley Anthologies*, *Avocet*, and a *Woody Guthrie Centennial Anthology*.

Mary Buchinger is the author of *Aerialist* (Gold Wake Press, 2015; shortlisted for the May Swenson Poetry Award, the OSU Press/The Journal Wheeler Prize for Poetry and the Perugia Press Prize). Her poems have appeared in *AGNI*, *Cortland Review*, *DIAGRAM*, *Fifth Wednesday*, *Nimrod International Journal of Prose and Poetry*, *The Massachusetts Review*, and elsewhere. She is Associate Professor of English and Communication Studies at MCPHS University in Boston, Mass. "Earrings I Never Wear" previously appeared in *Salamander*.

Matt Peters has an MFA in Creative Writing from the University of New Orleans. He currently teaches in the Creative Writing Department at Full Sail University and runs Beating Windward Press at BeatingWindward.com. "Hunters and Gatherers" is part of his collection *La Rue House*.

Melissa Grossman is an active member of Paradigm Poets in Los Angeles, CA, and Razor Babes, a performance troupe based in Ventura, CA. Melissa is a longtime student of Doraine Poretz, a member of her "Writing Down the Music of Your Life" workshop. Three of Melissa's poems are published in the anthology *In the Company of Women*. Her poetry has also been published in *Common Ground Review*, *Kansas City Voices*, *Askew*, *In the Spotlight*, *Quintessence Anthology 2008*, and *Windows Anthology 2010*.

Michael Dwayne Smith is editor-in-chief of Mojave River Press & Review. Recipient of both the Hinderaker Prize for poetry and the Polonsky Prize for fiction, his work appears in excellent journals like *Cortland Review*, *Word Riot*, *burntdistrict*, *San Pedro River Review*, *Stone Highway Review*, *Monkeybicycle*, *decomP*, and *>kill author*. His latest poetry collection, *Happy Good Time News*, is a collaboration with graphic novelist Evan Spears (forthcoming, Devils Hole Press, 2014). He lives near a ghost town in the Mojave Desert with his wife and rescued animals. Online he haunts MichaelDwayneSmith.com and MojaveRiverPress.com. "Andanza Motel, Anaheim, California" previously appeared in *MiCrow*.

Mickie Lynn revels in travel, reading, and the multifariousness of humanity. She enjoys expressing her artist self through writing, photography, and art. Her family, friends, little dog, and inner child make life more enriching. "Clean Water for Africa" is a winner of the 2014 Micah Challenge USA, Haikus for Clean Water contest. More Mickie Lynn can be found at: artistmickielynn.wordpress.com.

Nancy Scott is the managing editor of *U.S.1 Worksheets*, the journal of the U.S.1 Poets' Cooperative in New Jersey. Her most recent book, *Running Down Broken Cement* (Main Street Rag, 2014) is a collection of narrative poems inspired by her long career as a social worker for the State of New Jersey, a foster parent and an adoptive parent of three bi-racial children now adults. Visit her online at nancyscott.net. "Afghanistan, 2003"previously appeared in *Verse Wisconsin*, "Lost Boy of Sudan" previously appeared in *Out of Line*, "The Inheritance" previously appeared in *Liberty's Vigil* (The Occupy Anthology), and "Life after Welfare Reform" previously appeared in *Struggle*.

Nandini Dhar is the author of the chapbook *Lullabies Are Barbed Wire Nations* (Two of Cups Press, 2015). Her poems have recently appeared or are forthcoming in *Word Riot*, *Potomac Review*, *PANK*, *Los Angeles Review* and elsewhere. She is the co-editor of the journal *Elsewhere*. Nandini hails from Kolkata, India, and divides her time between her hometown and Miami, Florida, where she works as an Assistant Professor of English at Florida International University. "Midday Meal" previously appeared in *UCity Review*.

Odilia Galván Rodríguez, is an eco-poet, writer, editor, and activist, author of *Migratory Birds: New and Noted Poems*. She's worked as an editor for three magazines, most recently at *Tricontinental Magazine* in

Havana, Cuba. She facilitates creative writing workshops, and moderates Poets Responding to SB 1070 on Facebook.

Peggy Dobreer is a poet from Los Angeles. She studied yoga in India in 2008, and poetry in the Czech Republic in 2012. Her photos were taken on those journeys.

Phillip Larrea is the author of *We the People* (Cold River Press) and *Our Patch* (Writing Knights Press). Since 2012, his poems have appeared in over 70 journals, anthologies and magazines in the U.S., Ireland, Canada and Asia. He is the winner of the 2013 New Frontier Prize for poetry.

Rain Sheiman has an intense passion for life and for the people in it. Her carefree nature allows her to flourish in ways people may not understand. She looks through her lens with nature's eyes and has a humble, honest attitude towards others and herself. Her photographs reflect her fearlessness to stand up for what she believes in. And you might find her sharing a bottle of white wine around a fire while telling stories of humanity and adventure.

Raquel Reyes-Lopez is a fresh twenty-year-old Gemini. She is a member of the Whittier Poetry Group and assistant editor of *Cadence Collective*. She has poems published with *Bank-Heavy Press*, *East Jasmine Review*, *River's Voice*, *Kleft Jaw Press*, *Poetry in Motion*, and *San Gabriel Valley Poetry Quarterly*.

Ricki Mandeville is a freelance editor, public speaker, and language arts tutor whose poems have appeared in various journals, including *Comstock Review*, *San Pedro River Review*, *Penumbra*, *Texas Poetry Calendar 2014* and *2015*, and *Pea River Journal*. The author of *A Thin Strand of Lights* (Moon Tide Press), she lives and works near the ocean in Huntington Beach, CA.

Robert L. Woo is a psychotherapist with a Ph.D. in clinical psychology. He has written two film scripts, *Masquerade* and *Mirror Image*, and is currently working on his third. Besides writing, his other passions are playing tennis and encouraging his two daughters, a fashion designer and an accomplished writer, to follow their dreams.

Robert Jay lives in Long Beach where he also works as a longshoreman. He can often be found walking and biking the streets, discovering different routes, turning new corners, ever-vigilant and on the prowl for more poetry and photography material. Largely inspired by a short and minimalist writing style in the spirit of American Haiku, he writes of the subtle beauty of everyday life close to us. Personally trained by legendary Russian Strongmen, he also likes to practice random feats of strength to see just what he's capable of.

Robin Dawn Hudechek received her MFA in Creative Writing at UCI, and has taught writing at the university and college level for eleven years. Her poems have appeared in *Caliban*, *Cream City Review*, and in *Ghost Walk*, a chapbook. Currently, she is compiling her first full-length collection of poems.

Sadie Shorr-Parks is a nonfiction writer from Philadelphia. Her poetry and prose have appeared in *Blueline Literary Journal* and *Defunct Magazine*, among others. She has published book reviews with *The Iowa Review* and *The Southern Literary Review*. She currently teaches Composition and Rhetoric at West Virginia University.

Sharon Elliott was born and raised in Seattle and lives in Oakland. Four years in the Peace Corps in Nicaragua and Ecuador laid the foundation for her activism in multicultural women's issues. Her book, *Jaguar Unfinished*, was published in 2012. She was an awardee of the Best Poem of 2012, The Day of Little Comfort, by La Bloga On-Line Floricanto; and has been featured in poetry readings in the Bay Area. She is an initiated Lukumi priest of Scot/Sámi/African Carribbean ancestry, and an ally to people of color and to the earth.

Steve Ramirez hosts the weekly reading series Two Idiots Peddling Poetry and was one of the founders of the Orange County Poetry Festival. Publication credits include *Pearl*, *Crate*, *FreezeRay*, *Aim for the Head* (a zombie anthology) and *Multiverse* (a superhero anthology).

Susan Lefler is the author of *Brevard*, a photographic history (Arcadia Publishing, 2004), and of *Brevard, Then & Now* (Arcadia Publishing, 2012). Her first collection of poems, *Rendering the Bones*, was published by Wind Publications (2011) and won honorable mention in the 2012 Oscar Arnold Young Contest. She lives in Brevard, NC.

Suzanne Allen is a Pushcart Prize nominee, with poems published and anthologized in five countries and online at *Carnival*, *Cider Press Review*, *Hobo Camp Review* and *Crack the Spine*. She co-edits *The Bastille: The Literary Magazine of Spoken Word Paris*, creates poetry videos for Vlogosophy on YouTube, and her chapbook, *Verisimilitude*, is available at CorruptPress.org. "Keep Them All" was first published as an annual prize-winner in *California Quarterly* (2007) and has since appeared in *San Pedro River Review* and in *Villanelles: Everyman's Library* (Knopf, 2012)

Terry Wolverton is the author of ten books of poetry, fiction and creative nonfiction. She's the founder of Writers At Work, a creative writing studio in Los Angeles, and Affiliate Faculty in the MFA Writing Program at Antioch University, Los Angeles. www.terrywolverton.com. "The Secret of

Money" previously appeared in her most recent book, *Wounded World: Lyric Essays About Our Spiritual Disquiet.*

Terry Ann Wright recently received her MA from Goddard College. Her poetry has appeared recently or is forthcoming in *East Jasmine Review*, *The Fat City Review*, *The Altar Collective*, and *Cadence Collective*, and in the forthcoming *Cadence Collective: Year One Anthology*. She spends her days ridding the world of comma splices and her nights planning food-based road trips and sometimes writing.

Thomas R. Thomas was born in LA and grew up in West Covina and La Verne. He now lives in Long Beach, California. He works as a software QA Analyst. He volunteers for Tebot Bach. Thomas has been published in *Don't Blame the Ugly Mug: 10 Years of 2 Idiots Peddling Poetry*, *Creepy Gnome*, *Carnival*, *Pipe Dream*, *Bank Heavy Press*, *Conceit Magazine*, *Electric Windmill*, *Marco Polo*, and *Silver Birch Press Summer Anthology*. His books are *Scorpio* (Carnival), and *Five Lines* (World Parade Books). His website is thomasrthomas.org.

Timothy Matthew Perez was born and raised in Oxnard, California. He attended Cal State University, Long Beach, where he graduated in 1999 with an MFA in Creative Writing. He currently lives in Lake Elsinore and teaches English at Santiago High School in Corona.

Tobi Cogswell is a four-time Pushcart nominee and a Best of the Net nominee. Her sixth and latest chapbook is *Lapses & Absences* (Blue Horse Press). Her seventh chapbook, *The Coincidence of Castles*, is forthcoming from Glass Lyre Press. She is the co-editor of *San Pedro River Review* (www.sprreview.com). "Homeless Pete Gets Robbed on Catalina Avenue" previously appeared in *Hobo Camp Review* and "The Bench Outside the Thrift Store" previously appeared in *Steel Toe Review.*

Trista Dominqu was born and raised in the Southern California, where she continues to live with her husband and three children. Many times she sat upon brick walls dangling her legs, and though her parents were both hard workers, living paycheck to paycheck left days when cabinets had nothing to offer, but the trees around her did. "Leftover Orchard Days" first appeared in her chapbook *The Beauty of Muttliness* and relates to her real experiences of growing up in a city that was once home to hundreds of orange groves.

Viannah E. Duncan writes nonfiction by compulsion, poetry by inspiration, and reviews when the mood strikes. She holds an MFA in Creative Writing and has had her work published in several literary journals and anthologies. She has a cantankerous cat named Cleopatra with whom she's lived in California, Pennsylvania, and New York. For more, visit her website: duncanheights.com. "Widows" previously appeared in *Writer's Notes #5*.

Vincent Joseph Noto grew up in the San Joaquin Valley. In the 80s he had a poetry course from Philip Levine at CSU Fresno. For years Noto was a guerrilla teacher and tutor in Central and Southern California high schools and a bookstore manager. He now lives in Portland, Oregon. Noto's recent poetry can be found in *Connecticut River Review, Camel Saloon,* and *Contrary* magazines. He also writes creative nonfiction, has a short story forthcoming from Marin Poetry Center Press, and film criticism forthcoming from *The Luminary* (an online journal of Lancaster University, UK). Please visit: sites.google.com/site/vincentjosephnoto/

Yvonne M. Estrada is the author of the chapbook *My Name On Top of Yours*, a crown of sonnets and original photographs about graffiti in Los Angeles. Her poetry has appeared in *Mischief, Caprice & Other Poetic Strategies, Pulse Magazine, GuerrillReads.com, #8, Verse Wisconsin, 2011 Poem of the Month Calendar* and *Talking Writing*.

About the Editors

Nancy Lynée Woo is a poet, blogger, ghostwriter, editor and community organizer. After graduating from UC Santa Cruz with a degree in sociology, she was fortunate enough to have found a lovely poetry home in Long Beach, CA. Lucid Moose Lit was conceptualized in the fall of 2013 when realized she wanted to combine her two loves: social activism and poetry. Her poetry has been published in a few journals, such as *Synaethesia, Chaparral, Cadence Collective* and *Cease, Cows*. Her first chapbook, *Rampant,* is available now. If you'd like, you can follow her antics on Twitter @fancifulnance or peruse SpillTheInk.net.

Sarah Thursday calls Long Beach, California, her home, where she advocates for local poets and poetry events in her spare time from her other passion, teaching 4th and 5th graders. She runs a Long Beach-focused poetry website called CadenceCollective.net, co-hosts a monthly reading with one of her poetry heroes, G. Murray Thomas, and just started Sadie Girl Press as a summer job and way to help publish local and emerging poets. She just completed her first full-length poetry collection, *All the Tiny Anchors*. Find and follow her on SarahThursday.com, Facebook, or Twitter.

About the Cover Photographer

Mick Victor is a Los Angeles-based artist who shoots everything from abstract photography to portraits. The cover art and section photos are taken from the Art Unexpected project, in which the artist travels through the streets of big cities looking for special moments hidden in graffiti. The photographs used in this book are taken from the Teledyne series, and were shot in L.A. "I'm looking for the accidental images left behind where people paint walls, public facilities, and sidewalks. When they leave, someone often paints something else, and again and again on it goes. For me, the art is in the collision of everything unintended that happens and in chaos seems to become something quite beautiful in itself." The entire Art Unexpected series is stunning. You can see more at artunexpected.dphoto.com.

Thank You

We have so many people to thank for helping this project come to fruition. First, a resounding thank you to **Terry Wright** who helped us hone our selections and edit this book the entire way through. Her discerning eye and generous spirit provided exactly the right amount of perspective we needed to strike the balance we were aiming for.

Second, a warm thank you to our friend and collaborator **Mick Victor** for his beautiful photography, including both editors' author photos. Mick's artistic passion, love for his work and truly brilliant photography has been a special inspiration to this project.

Third, an ecstatic thank you to our Angel donor, **Michael Dwayne Smith** of **Mojave River Press and Review**. This generosity has encouraged the burning flame of this press in such a way that renders us eternally grateful.

We couldn't have even begun this journey without the never-ending support of our friends, family, and community. A special thanks to **Danielle Mitchell** of **The Poetry Lab** (where Sarah and Nancy first met). Thank you to **Alejandro Duarte** and **Raquel Reyes-Lopez** for lending their sharp eyes to the editing process of this book. A warm thanks to our community pillars— including **Gatsby Books**, **Half Off Books**, **WELabs**, **Viento Y Agua**—who have been there to hold space for projects like ours.

To all the people who make up the rich mosaic of our poetry community—you are the blood vessels of this beating heart we call home. Thank you to everyone who has lent a hand, a heart, a pair of reading eyes, a social media share or their precious time to encourage and help us complete this project. Especially, thank you to all our donors on IndieGoGo for helping us raise enough money to send this book to print. We couldn't do it without you all!

From Nancy: I would like to express a heartfelt thanks to **my father**, who has encouraged and supported my sometimes-doubtful foray into writing in these past few years. Your love and support means the world. A huge thank you to my godfather **Gary Reissman** for your unexpected gift of quite a large sum of money to help me get my car back at quite an ironic juncture in my life—I think this book expresses how much I appreciate it. To my girls, **Holly Carpenter** and **Alex Hattick**, you are true friends who have seen with your own eyes the actual amount of crazy it takes to chase after a dream.

Thank you for keeping me going. And of course, thank you **Sarah** for being a perfectly complementary kind of crazy in my life. You really do use your powers only for good; my love for you is enormous. Thank you to all the service organizations (**Shift Long Beach**, **Catalyst**, **Long Beach Time Exchange** and many, many more) in Long Beach for contributing your time and efforts to making our world a better place. Finally, thank you **Markus D. Manley** for spreading the seeds of inspiration and action; you will always be in my heart.

    From Sarah: Along with the previously mentioned support, I would like to include thanks to **my mom**, who believes in everything I do; my sister, **Renae**, who helped pushed me back into poetry; **Jeremiah** and **Terri**, my brother and sister-in-law; my nephew, **Josh**, and niece, **Kailani**, for just being. Also, **Alyssandra** and **Mickie**, who have slathered me with love and encouragement in all my insane projects and really helped me develop my new life motto, "Why not?" And **Nancy**. I love the see-saw propelling dance we do igniting and taming our mutual fire. I lost track of how many times our lack of words for describing the moment ends in crazy eyes, nodding heads, and a wild, "I know!"

Mojave River Press and Review

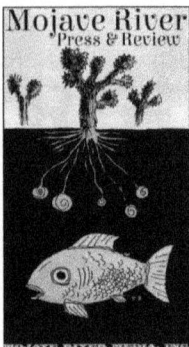

Mojave River Press and Review is proud to support Lucid Moose Lit's social justice literary projects. We encourage you to do likewise, however possible—contribute writing, purchase anthologies, offer volunteer hours, make financial contributions; working together creates meaningful help for people in need. We also encourage you to check out both the brilliant **Mojave River Press** book catalog and our eclectic literary journal, the **Mojave River Review**. We feature award-winning authors in poetry, fiction, and non-fiction, right alongside exciting new voices. You can find it all, including social media links, at MojaveRiverPress.com. Let's work together for better.

Love to all,
Michael Dwayne Smith
Publisher and Editor
Mojave River Press and Review